Fluent Influencing

Empowering Others to Follow Your Direction

Paul Archer

HH

High House Publishing

First published in Great Britain in 2016 by High House Publishing, Tivoli Studios, Cheltenham, Gloucestershire, GL50 2UG, United Kingdom.

Third Edition – Reprinted in 2022

Printed and bound in Great Britain by Lulu.com.

Copy edited by Angie Bruce and Grammarly

Cover designed by Shelley White

ISBN 978-0-9933112-2-2 (Paperback)

Contact Paul at:

paul@paularcher.com
www.paularcher.com

Table of Contents

This book is dedicated to Lewis, Euan, Jessica, Shelley and Bethan, who have all mastered the art of influencing me.

Why's Influencing so Important?

Algo's and Robots

Are you protected from the robots?

There's been a lot of talk of robo-advisers and computer algorithms taking over jobs in the future. In my last book, I wrote about the rise of automated intelligence and how this will match the old industrial revolution in its capability to swamp jobs.

The old Luddites of the cotton mills may be returning.

But let's see if your favourite vocation is threatened.

Research by Oxford University calculated that from 700 job descriptions, ranging from dentists to financial advisers, more than a third will go to robots or AI within a decade.

That's scary.

But the good news is they found that if you want to keep your job, you want one that requires:

- Creativity
- Durable empathy skills
- The ability to influence people
- Anything involving handling people

Because computers, algorithms, and AI can't do that yet. Well, maybe not in my lifetime.

So are you protected from the robots?

Behavioural Economics

There's nothing wrong with influencing.

Because it works. And it's all about results.

The British Government took a gamble in 2010. Like all governments, they need to encourage citizens to pay taxes, follow the laws and modern administrations like to embolden us to live longer, stop smoking and take exercise.

In the past, they used public information films with limited success.

But in 2010, David Cameron set up the BIT – Behavioural Insights Team. Using psychology and various methods of subtle or hypnotic influencing, they improved the results of over 150 projects.

The one I liked was inspiring people to donate organs by using the principle of reciprocity – "You'd be happy to have a transplant if you needed one, so why not help others?"

BIT was a complete success.

So use some inducing techniques, and you need to go no further than reading Cialdini's principles of influencing and adapting the methods spoken about in the book to your everyday work and life. It's all about results.

Let's Clear Up What We Mean by Influencing

How to Influence Today's Knowledge Worker?

Brodie and Florence are my two Italian Spinone dogs and like to be told what to do. They will obey their master's voice. But fellow humans don't.

Nobody wants to be told what to do; customers don't want to be presented with old-style sales techniques that push features and benefits. The modern knowledge worker will not tolerate being told, particularly the younger generation – our Generation Ys. Everyone wants "buy-in" and involvement when it comes to decisions; modern firms ensure engagement.

So how do we influence your customers, team members and colleagues?

Let me explain how.

Firstly, fathom out what your intentions are when it comes to influencing. Do you genuinely want the person to go with your idea or force them to accept it? Then decide if it's influencing what you want to do because there are four choices here. To:

Persuade – here, you will change their minds and convince them of the idea through your willpower. It's not always successful and is fairly short term. Persuading is overt, i.e. using techniques that can be clearly seen coming and often avoided by savvy customers. It can be seen as "pushy" or controlling if done in a clumsy manner.

Manipulate – this is deceitful, controlling and directing. You leave them with little choice. It creates a negative emotion and definitely will be short term. It leaves people bruised.

Negotiate or create a win: win. Both parties win, but this normally involves some compromise.

Influence – now we're getting there. Influencing helps the customer to change their feelings about something. You win over their minds but also their hearts; they will voluntarily change their mind. Long term but can take a whole lot longer to achieve. It is covert; in other words, it relies on methods that are not clearly seen, often dealing with the subconscious or influencing on a subconscious level. It's subtle.

Let me show you how you can influence. We're all aware that people make decisions on an emotional level and then justify that decision in a more logical fashion. There have been plenty of studies proving this. The point is that we need to appeal to people's emotions rather than their logic or rational brain.

The Sonos Speakers and the Subtle Art of Selling

I love my music, always have. As a 13-year-old, I'd save two weeks' wages from my paper-round to buy an album – The Stranglers, The Cure, Siouxsie and the Banshees – seminal favourites.

I really couldn't afford to buy much music in the '80s and '90s – with CDs retailing at £18 in 1994, I struggled to justify buying Blur's Parklife, but some things you'll sacrifice eating for.

Music got free in 2000 (a great book by way of the same title), things changed, and for the rest of the decade, I gorged on all the music I could find. Then I discovered festivals and my favourite of all time is the Glastonbury Festival – the world's best.

However, incredibly challenging to buy tickets, and I have failed to go more times than I've been. This year was no exception, so I thought I'd treat myself to ward off the disappointment.

I signed up for Spotify and bought 6 Sonos One Speakers for our new house. Now, if you haven't experienced Sonos speakers and Spotify, you haven't lived, especially if you're into your music like I am.

I bought them on a whim – over a grand for speakers – how on earth could I justify the cost?

That's precisely how consumers buy. The emotions help them to open up their wallets, but as they walk out of the store or exit the shopping cart online, they need a logical reason to justify the purchase. Good salespeople arm the customer with valid reasons once the sale has been completed to prevent cancellations and the cooling-off notice. Do you?

People buy on emotion and justify the cost on logic.

My speakers were bought because I was disappointed on missing out on Glastonbury again. I was on a low and needed an emotional pickup.

Logically they allow me to listen to great tunes, to hear practically any song I choose. I've attached Alexa to them, so I don't need to buy Amazon's tinny speakers, and she's excellent at getting us up in the morning with her alarm. The cost was pretty much the same as Glasto would have been for a long weekend's break.

If you don't know what a grand is, then you're probably not from the UK. "A Grand Don't Come for Free" Who was the band? Answers on a postcard, please.

Pace, Pace, Pace and Some More Pace

So how do we present to the emotional part of people's brains? We bring in a little NLP – Neuro-Linguistic Programming – and yes, you can get jabs for that from chemists. NLP is a really cool set of tools for communicating with people and influencing is known simply as pace, pace, pace and lead.

Many persuaders or influencers fail because they lead too quickly. Leading is the convincing bit, showing the idea and promoting the benefits. This is too soon and is the reason why customers or team members will withdraw or disagree with your idea. You led too soon.

Pacing is getting on their level, observing physiology, understanding their world, building a strong rapport, seeing the argument from their side, working out what values and motives the person has, what makes them "tick". Being intently curious achieves this. Leading involves suggesting, moving, and proposing your idea. But remember, don't do this too soon.

NLP has lots of technical terms to describe these things – mirroring, meta-programmes, calibration, neuro levels, anchoring, criteria elicitation and hypnosis – but fret not, I'm not going to refer to these too much; just explain how you can use the tools to influence – to pace, pace, pace and lead.

Now we know what modern influencing is all about, we can get on with learning how to do it even more.

And my two dogs, perhaps I could start using some of these tools to influence them rather than persuade them? I wonder how they would react with "Brodie, how much pleasure would it give you for you to come here with me?" Maybe not. "Brodie…come".

Influencing Emotionally

Why is it that people insist on making buying decisions based on emotion? And afterwards, they try every angle to justify the decision. Read on to see what you can do about this to help your influencing.

The school holidays have just begun here in the Archer household, which has coincided with influencing 9 puppies that Brodie gave birth to last month. It's been a long haul, creating blogs, and photos on the sites, taking phone calls, and talking to prospective owners. So far we've found brilliant homes for 6 pups, and do you know what the secret to influencing the puppies is?

Quite simple. You sit the family down on the couch and you put a puppy in their arms. 5 minutes later, they've fallen in love and want to keep it. I used to call this technique the "puppy dog close". To sell anything, let the customer feel what it's like to own it. Pet shop owners would give the customer the puppy to take home for the weekend, knowing full well, that by Monday morning, they would want to own it.

Emotions taking over. And we created the same thing, inadvertently, by letting the owner cuddle their new puppy. You see, puppies are devastatingly cute. You can't resist their little noses, their big brown eyes and tiny tails wagging for you. Puppies have an in-built ability to just love you and be with you. And that's far too much emotion for most humans to resist.

So when my wife announced that she wanted to keep not one puppy for us…but two pups, I was astonished and immediately my logic cells kicked in.

She was all emotional and was soon allied by three children, all oozing uncontrollable, irrational decision making. "Daddy, we have to keep Alfie and Florence."

Why is having three dogs an irrational decision:

1. Italian Spinones grow up to be very large and hairy dogs, and puppies grow up, believe me.

2. We don't have room for three dogs in the boot of the car.

3. It'll be me who has to walk them. Now walking one dog is easy; Brodie runs with me; two dogs seem OK, but walking three huge Spinones seems impossible.

4. Vets fees for 3 dogs require a new credit card and make my eyes water.

5. So does 3 pet insurance plans; Brodie costs me £30 a month.

6. And think of the food costs!

7. And there are the kennel fees if we go away.

My family are still clouded in emotion and desperately wants to keep 2 puppies as well as Brodie.

The lesson? Think about what you sell. Are you making the purchasing decision emotional?

- If you sell photos of sports events, do you play on the emotional memories that you can take away and recall forever….or do you focus on the 5" x 4" photo being of good quality and high resolution and easily uploaded to Facebook?

- If you sell life insurance, do you focus on the features and bolt-ons, the low monthly premiums…or do you talk about the inner warm feeling that if anything ever happened to you, your family would never have to think bad thoughts over your grave? Money, or the lack of it, changes people.

- Do you ask questions to reveal the emotional needs and pains of the customer?

- When influencing the house, do you ask where little Johnnie's room might be and how would he decorate it? Remember the puppy dog close.

- Do you ask what it might feel like to own the product, what it might mean to them….play on the emotions?

- Do you play on your sales team's emotions when influencing or persuading them? Most decisions have emotion packed into them, even when you're not buying anything.

- If you don't then you really ought to.

So where does this emotional buying decision leave me? When I pick up Florence and Alfie, yes my family have already named them, I just adore them, who wouldn't, they're puppies. But logically, I think it's wrong and I genuinely need your help.

Let's Catch up With Our Customer First

Calibrate First

A few years ago, I was pulled over by the boys in blue, the police as we call them here in the UK. I hadn't done anything wrong, although I felt strangely guilty. It's how they handle you. And I knew what they were going to do first.

That's right, calibrate me.

You see like it or not, if your state changes, so does your physiology – your body language. They say there is a "tell" for everything and as a modern influencer, being able to read your customer's physiology is essential so you can understand their state of mind and pace them to an influencing position.

And my new police friend was about to do that by asking me some "yes" and "no" questions. He wanted to observe my physiology which is why he asked me to step out of the car because he wanted to observe my whole body language.

I also knew he'd have been trained on using his peripheral vision. Normally we use what's called foveal vision or looking straight into people's eyes – it's years of conditioning but when you're influencing, you really want to get good at peripheral vision. My new friend was.

And he began to ask me a series of questions requiring a "yes" and a "no" answer because he wanted to calibrate my physiology for a yes and a no. The reason? Quite simply, because when the real question came in, he wanted to gauge whether I was lying or not. Clever.

Try it yourself. Find someone you know. Ask them to think firstly of someone they don't like, observe their physiology. Now ask them to think of someone they like a lot, observe their physiology and note the difference. You've calibrated them. In influencing or influencing you can now use this to present an idea to them, if they like it, you'll see it in their physiology without even asking them. Useful.

You could ask your customer or person you want to influence about sometime recently when they successfully bought something or took on someone's idea. Just make it casual conversation. Observe and calibrate them and then move the conversation onto a purchase that didn't work out. Observe, spot the difference and now you have the key.

I sell training and consultancy and I normally ask my prospective clients about training they've bought in the past that really worked out and then training that didn't. Naturally, I'm listening to what they're saying, but carefully calibrating their physiology because I want to see the same buying signals when I make my presentation.

By the way, it was my rear fog light being on in clear visibility. I just reckon he was bored.

How Do People Tick?

Now onto how people "tick" or as NLP calls it – meta-programs. A horrible word that. These are deep-rooted mental programs which direct our thought processes. In other words, how we "tick". Have a look at this picture:

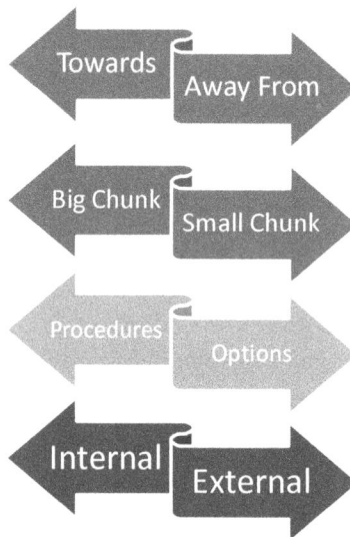

These are the four that we can spot with physiological clues thus allowing us to covertly recognise people's motivation before we even attempt to influence them.

Towards – Away From

Someone's motivation is either generally towards a goal or an objective or some pleasure or away from pain or discomfort. This one is especially useful in influencing because you can pitch your idea either helping them to achieve a goal or move away from some pain or issue.

Look for your subject's body leaning forward, check the spine, it will lengthen as they move forward. The opposite is true for an away from person – they will move backwards and their spine will shrink.

Big Chunk – Small Chunk

Chunk size determines how big a picture people are. If they are big picture people, preferring to look at strategy rather than the detail, they will be big chunk. Small chunk people like the detail and minutiae of the subject.

Look for gestures. Large sweeping gestures will hint to a big chunker and small, precise gestures will show a small chunk person.

Procedures – Options

Procedures people like order, lists, the right way to approach things or the established order. Options people are opposites. They like choice, variety, new ways of doing things.

Look for their direction of their time line. Procedures people will demonstrate time in front of them; they will show this with their gestures sweeping left to right in front indicating an order for things. First, second and third point being shown with gestures along a line in front.

Options people will have a time line behind them and in front with gestures randomly placed. You can easily spot a procedures person, if you don't, chances are they are options.

Internal – External

Internal people operate individually creating their own energy and motivation from inside. They don't need external sources to create momentum. Externals do. They need people or other external features to provide the energy and drive to exist.

Internals can be spotted because they are normally still – few gestures or body movement. Externals can be the opposite, gracious gestures, and wide body movement, with inclusive gestures.

Your peripheral vision will pick up these clues and with them you can gauge their colour and how they "tick".

Customers Will Strive to Avoid Pain

Have you noticed how many diet products there are on the market right now? Even Tesco's Supermarket is promoting its online diet. And have you noticed how they are marketing it to people? Are they focussing on losing weight, trimming inches or are they focussing on a new you, a slimmer figure?

Research from Minnesota University in late 2008 has shown that the buying public is more concerned with trying to avoid pain when buying products or services than anything else. In fact, over 80% of the people they interviewed were avoiding issues, problems and pains rather than striving for some goal.

Maybe this is to do with the current down-economy or the way people naturally are, but it certainly helps us when we're influencing.

Think about it. People will do anything to avoid real or perceived pain or to rid themselves of problems, and this is a massive motivator. NLP calls it towards and away from. People are motivated either as towards things such as goals or away from things like pain.

So a diet product will appeal to people differently. Towards people will want to have a slimmer figure, get a partner or look good on the beach naked.

Away from people will buy a diet product if it helps them lose weight, stop having tight-fitting trousers, stop wearing unfashionable clothes, to stop people staring at them or feeling sorry for them.

Think of the last thing you bought. Was it an away from or a towards purchase? I bought some running shoes last autumn because my old ones were worn out and hurting my toes – I didn't want that pain anymore. I bought BUPA medical insurance because I didn't want to worry about having to wait for an operation, and if truth be told, I didn't want my wife moaning at me anymore that we didn't have private insurance.

The difference is clear and it also helps us to look at the way we sell our products, services and ideas, and the key lesson is that 80% of people are away from buyers. So dust off your products and services and examine how they prevent pain. Find out what troubles your customer's experience. Do some research, run some focus groups, ask them, and get your marketing department to find out what problems your products fixes. Forget about benefits and features, that's so noughties, and focus on away from pain solving.

And me…I had a good Christmas so I definitely need to buy some diet products so these trousers don't feel so tight. Has anyone got the Tesco Diet web address?

Walking in Your Customer's Shoes

I have two sons separated by 2 years, very similar in looks but you couldn't get two different characters. One is reserved, effortlessly sensitive, worries about people all the time and can spot a personal feeling a mile away even in camouflage.

My other son is completely oblivious to people's feelings, beliefs and opinions and is always the centre of attention and very talkative. Not that he's a bad boy, just different.

I know which one is going to be the natural influencer.

You see influencers, coaches, team leaders, sales support teams all need to be sensitive to other people's situations, they need to show empathy to customers' positions in order to gain rapport and sell successfully. Empathy can be defined as knowing how people think, and what's going on in their world without necessarily agreeing with them. And I firmly believe that this skill can be learnt, so there is hope for my son.

There are two steps to having empathy with customers.

1.   Step one is being aware of their situation.
2.   Step two is acknowledging that you are aware.

Remember to go to step two as people can't guess that you understand them; you have to make it known.

Here are 9 practical tips to turn up your empathy volume by being aware of their situation and then showing that you're responsive.

Read between the lines.

I call this level 3 or global listening – it's the ability to read what's not been said, to rely on gut reactions, to use your sixth sense, to use your intuition. That way, you can understand where the customer is coming from. Level 1 and 2 listening is as far as most of us go – level 1 is selfish listening in that everything you hear gets related to your personal experiences and for your own purposes. Level 2 is listening or active listening and appreciating your customer's point of view.

Trust your level 3. Trust your intuition to read between the lines.

Non-verbal clues

Or body language. To be really empathetic, you need to be able to read body language so you can read beyond what is being said. People can change the words they use, but they can't hide their body language. Look for clusters of gestures, not isolated ones.

For example, crossed arms might be because they're cold or are hiding their paunch. It may not mean being negative or hostile. But crossed arms, alongside crossed body and legs, sitting behind a barrier, jerky eye contact and pacier language would normally mean there's something up in their mind, and it's not good.

Lower your voice tone

A lower voice pitch is more empathetic. Learn to deepen your tone and people will warm to you sooner. Do ensure your vocals have a good range though; no one wants to listen to someone who is monotone in their delivery.

Listen more

Most influencers appreciate this, but three things you can do to listen with empathy are to paraphrase, mirror language and use silence more. Paraphrasing asks that you use the customer's language and words when summarising. Occasionally repeat back one or two words and raise your voice as you say them to indicate a subtle question. This will get the customer to say more. And silence is the best way to let your customer say how it is, especially on the phone. I always believe that phone operators would become comfortable with a few seconds of silence so long as there is a purpose to this.

Tell stories

Tell stories during your influencing. Use stories to prove your expertise, to demonstrate your product's uniqueness; in fact, any part of the sales process can be enlivened with a story. Now when you tell a story, a strange thing happens in the customer's mind. They translate the story into their world as if they were in the story. This helps to show them that you are like them, that you share similar ideals. People love a story, it's something granted to us as children, and we never lose the irresistibility of a tale.

Rapport

It is having something in common with someone, where you are both in tune with each other and can see each other's point of view. You just seem to get on. This normally happens over time. You know when you're with a friend because silence doesn't feel uncomfortable; you just feel relaxed. Friends have deep rapport – they share many aspects of their lives. They think the same much of the time, have things in common, laugh together and often move in line in more ways than they think.

Rapport is something you can accelerate with customers to help build empathy. The quickest and easiest way to do this is to deliberately become like them in some subtle ways. Learn to match them in physical ways. Mirror their body language, and positioning; match their voice pace and tone; do this subtly and don't mimic. It's definitely worth practising as it does work.

Empathy gestures

Showing empathy with your body language is something that women are far better at than men. My daughter, who is 8 next month, has this completely tied up. She knows when to turn on the empathy charm with Daddy to get what she wants.

One of her weapons is head tilt. Bethan uses this when she wants to show lots of empathy for my situation and simply tilts her head sideways. This has a magical effect on the person talking and shows deep empathy.

Try this yourself.

Other empathy creating gestures are smiles, eye contact, open body language, and hands to face to indicate deep listening and thinking about your situation.

Reflective statements

These are really useful little phrases that tell your customer that you see where they're coming from. You may not necessarily agree with them but you appreciate their point of view. That's empathy and not being a "yes" man or woman. Some examples:

- "I understand what you're saying."
- "I can appreciate how you feel about that."
- "I've been through that as well, and it was terrible."
- "I see where you're coming from."
- "Gosh that must be awful."

So there we have my 9 tips to show more empathy with your customer – a particularly important skill for influencers or anyone who deals with people as part of their profession. Some people are natural at it – most of us have to learn it – these 9 tips can help you do just that.

Client Influencing Stories

Have you ever attended a Speed Networking event? Fabulous idea, naturally, where likeminded business professionals have 2 minutes to tell each other about their services and products.

Unfortunately they can become very "samey", with everyone spouting out their value propositions and elevator pitches. We've heard it all before.

An alternative is to develop client influencing stories. These mini stories are designed to influence people on a subconscious level, to understand in under a minute, exactly what value you provide to your clients.

The secret is to keep them to a minute and to follow the age old steps to crafting the story. Let me give you an example, then I'll unpack what I did.

Colin and Debi

Colin was a hard worker, totally dedicated to his young wife Debi. He was a railway worker eagerly completing his apprenticeship. He had ambitions to be a train driver and was looking forward to starting a family as soon as they could afford to.

Debi and Colin were in their early 20s, newly married, and that day, were celebrating their first year's wedding anniversary. It was a cold November day, Colin was working late, keen to get home for Debi's surprise meal, which he knew about, after all, Debi had given him a huge number of hints. Colin was tall, over 6 feet, strong and totally in love with her.

The evening fog had descended on the rail yard, Colin's last job that evening was to guide two locomotives into the sidings, couple them together and then get off for home.

He used a night light system designed to give train drivers instructions on the same basis as traffic lights. Colin was experienced in this procedure and had just indicated to the first driver to hold still whilst he crossed the tracks to show the second driver to begin coming forward.

Whether the first driver hadn't seen the light or he was half asleep, was irrelevant as the solid steel coupling device took the life out of Colin instantly.

One year later, Debi had begun to socialise once again and had returned to work on a part-time basis, not for the money, but for the need to continue her life. The life assurance policy I'd sold them paid off their mortgage completely and gave Debi a lump sum that gave her the ability to never worry about money again and to rebuild her life.

The 4 steps to follow

A true story which occurred early in my career as a life assurance salesman, and yes, I've told the story many times.

The story clearly lays out the value I provided at the time to customers, mixes emotions with visual imagination and can be told in under one minute.

It follows these steps:

1. Scene and characters

2. Journey

3. Obstacle

4. Solution

Can you recall the character Colin? And the scene? Late November, happy married young couple, 6 foot tall Colin.

The journey…coupling the trains in the foggy evening. The obstacle…coupling successfully so he could return home for a romantic meal.

The solution…life assurance that allowed Debi never to worry about money again.

The client influencing story has many uses. You can use them with customers when you want to influence them to take out a product, or introduce the value you provide. You can also use them with your introducers.

Many of my clients rely on bank or building society staff to provide leads and telling these stories to them is a powerful way of illustrating what you do.

People remember emotions and can imagine the scene, so powerful in influencing them.

Wouldn't they also be useful when speed networking as well? It would certainly prevent the yawns.

How to Get Along with Everyone

I was Stateside earlier this year running a week-long sales management workshop in Miami. We had a ball, the group warmed to my Brit sense of humour, and we enjoyed a week of prime development. We all got along fine from day one, which made the whole process so much more enjoyable. One of my skills is to get on with almost any group of people.

On the flight back across the Atlantic, I was pondering how important it is for salespeople to quickly "get on" with customers to smooth the process. And in Terminal 3 Bus Station, awaiting my coach back to Cheltenham, I realised I have an empathy with all types of people.

The ability to get on with almost anyone is a skill which can be learnt. Here are some ideas:

- Find common ground immediately. Look for clues if you're in the customer's home or office.

- Have a sense of humour. Nothing draws people towards you than a cheery disposition. If you have a default angry face, then change it.

- Read widely especially current affairs. I pick up three magazines each week – The Economist, The Week and Money Week. This gives me an unbridled knowledge of what's going on. In the USA, I could chat about Donald Trump, the Republican Party, Joe Biden, Congress and the Fed's increase in interest rates with confidence.

- Follow the English Football Premiership; this will allow you to start a conversation with most men in the UK. Supporting Manchester United often gets a laugh. Knowledge of the Rugby Premiership also adds value.

- Mirror the customer's energy level.

- Talk about people's journey to the office or venue.

- Know the latest movies at the cinema.

- Have an affinity for people's hobbies, exercise routines and past-times.

- If abroad, research the nation's sport. In the USA, I spoke about baseball and American Football and the Super Bowl.

- Keep away from religion in your conversation.

I know it's not essential for the customer to like you; after all, you're a sales professional, but if you can get on with almost anyone, you'll do more business. Period. Or is it a full-stop?

Syncing

Begin mirroring with the handshake.

We mostly all shake hands with our customers. Of course we do, but do you use this as an opportunity to start calibrating your customer and begin the mirroring process?

Offer your hand by subtly moving it from your side by about 6 inches; this is a very subliminal gesture for the other person to shake your hand, but enough not to get embarrassed if they don't.

Shake and measure their pace and get in tune with their rhythm at this stage. Calibrate their pace and match it. Match their squeeze and tempo of the shake.

On the subject of tempo, continue to gauge them as a person and match their pace, energy, voice and personality. Match their language and use their words, their preferred language and style. Find out their hot buttons i.e. how they tick; know what's important to them.

Immerse yourself in them.

Mimic no, mirror yes.

Sit down with your back to the wall, if you can, with nothing to distract them, say a blank wall, open up your body language, engage them with hypnotic eye contact and begin your sales induction.

You can only ever begin the influencing once you have established a rapport – hypnotic influencing is not about being best buddies but changing your manner to adapt to your customer's approach.

Think like them, behave like them, speak like them, know what makes them tick and you'll then be ready for the influencing. But haven't you already started influencing?

We mentioned earlier that people like people who are like themselves. It may not be fair, but it is certainly true. We choose our friends, partners and acquaintances from those people who view things in the same way as we do.

One of the surest and often quickest methods to build a rapport with your customer is to match them physically. This is well known and documented and many people get it wrong, make fools of themselves and stop doing it. It needs to be subtle and natural and then it works. It really does work.

Matching Posture

Match general posture and positioning, not each and every arm movement. Observe your client carefully and gradually move your posture to match theirs. Lean back, sideways or whatever is appropriate to mirror them. Don't worry about arm movements or crossing of limbs – just go for the basic posture.

Matching Energy Levels

Then match pace. Are they fast and energetic or slow and cumbersome? Match your pace alongside theirs. More or less of the coffee helps here! Seriously though, have you ever dealt with someone who has a naturally slow pace?

Hard work, isn't it? And vice versa too. But when we're dealing with someone at the same pace, it makes the meeting so much more fruitful.

Matching Pace

More experienced matchers then go for breathing patterns and match these. This is a great way to ensure you are able to match their pace as well since the two go together.

Have you ever been in a crowd of people singing a chant or a song? Maybe at a rock concert singing along to the chorus? Think back now and just know that whilst you sing, your breathing patterns are like everyone else's and a phenomenal rapport exists in the crowd.

Matching Voice

Then comes voice. There's so much you can do to match people's voice and when you're on the telephone, this is pretty much all you can match. Try to match their voice speed and tone. Do they speak high or low? Try it. It does produce a very amicable conversation between two like-minded people.

Match their Voice to Maximise Rapport

One of my favourite accents comes from Southern Louisiana, USA. Slow, drawling, and rhythmic. Try to copy it, and it sounds terrible. Like the Ant Hill Mob driver in the Whacky Races or Tinker in Speed Buggy. YouTube both of those that if you don't remember.

This person, probably from New Orleans, has grown up with others from the same area who sound the same or comparable. Their parents appeared similar and probably gave them their accent in the first place. So, for them to hear an identical voice must be nectar for their ears.

We can't and mustn't imitate an accent – that's mimicry.

But we can match the voice. Three areas to match.

1.   Volume or loudness.

2.   Pace or speed.

3.   Resonance or deepness.

The trick is to listen carefully, and fathom out where their voice comes from. Does it emanate from the throat? Kind of nasally.

Or from the top of the stomach.

Or from deep below, under the stomach. Resonant and deep like a trombone.

Now make your voice come from the same place, and you'll be amazed how accurately you'll begin the match their sound without mimicking them at all.

High up in the throat – fast and high pitched. Low down, deep in the abdomen, is low timbre and slow. The middle of the stomach is medium paced and toned. Try it; it works.

Do this, and the person you're talking to will feel right at home rather than talking to a stranger.

Or was it Penelope Pitstop from Wacky Races? Now there's a blast from the past, and Peter Perfect was always on hand to rescue that lil ol' lady.

Life's a Rollercoaster

I've never travelled on a rollercoaster. Honest, I know it sounds remarkable, but I've never had the courage to climb in the small cab and ride the heart wrenching and stomach-churning experience.

Until one afternoon over Christmas when my youngest son dared me to get on the ride at Poulton's Park. Now if you ever want to motivate me to do something, you only need to dare me. I think it's hard-wired into most men.

I watched Euan first and thought I'd use the 1st, 2nd, and 3rd position that we use all the time when influencing. Now, this clever little tip helps you see, feel and fully understand what it's like for someone else and in sales, is a really useful way of exploring the customer's point of view.

1st position is where you look at things through your own eyes and as I stared at Euan on the rollercoaster all I could think of was fear, trepidation, how foolish, help!

2nd position is where you step out of your shoes and move into the customer's shoes and look at things through this person's eyes; in other words see and feel their point of view. So I tried this and moved into Euan's shoes. Initially, I could still feel my fear and trepidation, but I kept at it and began to see how Euan saw the ride. He was smiling and cheering, so loud I could hear him from where I was standing. As he approached the top of the loop just before he was to plunge downwards at breath-taking speed, his look was of apprehension but total excitement. He was enjoying the thrill of the ride and I started to feel what this was like for him.

3rd position is where you stand back, disassociate yourself from both viewpoints and look objectively at the situation. With customers, we get to see their views and yours in tandem. On the rollercoaster, I could see Euan's viewpoint, mine and the other passengers on the coaster. I realised that everyone seemed to be having fun and that this miserable father was seeing the rollercoaster in a very blinkered way.

And did I enjoy it? Yes, I did, and I had to go on it again and again. In fact since it wasn't too busy I went on the same ride 3 times and Euan now thinks his Dad is real cool.

So next time you really want to appreciate your customer's point of view, go from 1st position to 2nd and then finally to 3rd position.

Learn To Focus on The Face

I'm on a flight right now as I write, and the steward has enormously animated facial expressions, so I match them and we're getting on fine.

I think though, we're reluctant to look at the face as much as we ought to. With the advent of video technology allowing us to commonly communicate to each other with video screens, the emphasis on the face is only going to increase.

By reading the expressions, the movements, and the micro-expressions, we can learn more about what the customer is really thinking than traditional body language, which focuses on gestures and voice.

The problem is that we're brought up not to look at the face too much, it's a sign of rudeness, so we need to get over this.

My message today is to learn to focus more on people's faces when we communicate, and that way, we can open the doors to a better understanding of facial expressions. Start the next time you do a video conference.

Believe me; this will become a number one skill in the future for face to face influencers.

Only when we become comfortable in looking at people's faces in more detail can we master the art of interpreting micro-expressions, but that's for another day.

Rapport is Common Ground

A couple of years ago I lived on a typical family estate with 3 and 4 bedroom homes, each with three children, two dogs and one barbeque. Every November I received a box of poppies from the Royal British Legion and I would knock on doors to see how many poppies I could sell.

Each year I raised a consistent £35 or so.

People weren't reticent about buying poppies; after all, it's an amazing cause. The problem was that many people had already bought their poppy or had signed up for a standing order or always bought one from a favourite seller. So I had to be happy with my £35.

But one year I decided on a different tactic and thought about building a rapport with my customers. At the time, my son Lewis was aged 5 and actually rather cute. He's now turned into a teenager, so is now rather frightening.

I decided to take him with me so I decked him out with the posters of rank, a box of poppies around his waist and a cute bobble hat.

And what happened next was amazing.

The first door I knocked on, the man of the house came to the door, looked at me and quickly realised that I was selling poppies, then he glanced at Lewis and I could read the man's mind.

"Ah", he thought, "this man is selling poppies...I already have my poppy...how can I turn him down? But hold on...he has a son about the age of my son...he's a dad like me...we have something in common...I like this man...he's just like me...where's my wallet?"

That night I made £78.50. Same road, same houses, same people. But I doubled my takings.

The simple fact was that I was showing my customers that I was the same as them; I was building a common ground. You see people like to deal with people who are the same as them and have done so for thousands of years.

It may not be fair but it's true. People like to deal with people who are the same as them.

The first thing they teach you in sales training school is to find something in common with your customer and talk about this. In fact, Dale Carnegie made this famous in his book "How to Make Friends and Influence People" which was one of the first nonfiction books (outside of college) I ever read.

Something else you can easily do is to become more like your customer and the way they are. Pick up on one or two aspects of them and match these. This will build a strong initial rapport.

When face to face with customers, we can pick up on their body language, seating position, gestures, eye contact, energy levels, conversation…and copy one or two of these. Don't make it too obvious, maybe have a time-lapse of a few seconds. Possibly sit like they are sitting and copy the amount of eye contact they give you and slow down or speed up to match their energy levels.

When not face to face, on the telephone, you can pick up on aspects of their voice such as speed, volume, tone, and rhythm.

Try to follow a couple of aspects of their voice, such as their pace and maybe their tone. You'll be amazed as to the effect it'll have. Your customer will feel you are a little like them and will warm up to you more.

With a rapport built, you can then concentrate on influencing.

The Social Styles Colours

Gauge Your Customer First

In influencing and coaching, sometimes you just have to break the rules and adapt to the situation.

Last week I went to see an important new prospect for the first time. I'd secured a meeting via a prospecting call and hadn't actually met him. So I thought I'd phone his Personal Assistant to see how to approach him. This is an excellent tip in its own right.

The PA was quite happy to tell me about her boss once I persuaded her that this would mean her boss would get more value from the meeting and I wouldn't take up more time than was necessary.

I use a neat system to categorise people – it's based around four colours – red people, blue, green and yellow people. This comes from an excellent piece of kit called the Social Styles which I use all the time. It helps you to understand where people are coming from and how to handle them for maximum influence.

From her description of her boss I soon realised he was very red. Red people want to get to the point, they want you to be very professional with inbuilt credibility, of course they want politeness – who doesn't – but they don't want chit chat. Be confident with them and self-assured but don't shine above them. Talk revenue and profit and value statements. Don't thank them for their time – your time is just as valuable. Talk goals and vision and big picture. And above all be prepared as they will test you and check your ability and credibility. They want and demand results.

Sure enough he turned out like this and, thankfully, I was well prepared and answered his questions. We got straight down to business and exchanged no pleasantries apart from shaking hands. The need to build a rapport and a relationship would happen during the business discussion. The atmosphere was right for him.

In the present business market, we influencers should make the most of every meeting we get.

So next time you have a meeting with a new prospect or customer, find out about them beforehand or quickly gauge the kind of person they are when you meet them. Tailor your approach accordingly.

How Does Colouring in Clients Help Influencers?

I'm going to show you a very simple yet powerful way of colouring in your buyer so you can adapt your selling to suit them and become a little bit like them, borrowing some of their traits.

You see the basis of rapport is that people like to deal with people who are a little like them. So borrowing some of their mannerisms and characteristics is a pure complement to your customer.

The secrets that I'm going to share with you right now will allow you to quickly identify the customer and sell to them the way they want to buy. That's really customer focussed selling.

OK, so what are the secrets to colouring in your buyer? The first thought is that everyone we meet is different. Everyone is bristling with emotions, ways, priorities, and behaviours and no one human is the same as the next.

The Social Styles is a tool that we can use to provide clues as to who we really are. The four different colours describe four different types of people, four different values, four different motivations and drivers. More than anything else though, the Social Styles is remarkably accurate and sublimely straightforward to understand and a knowledge and application of this will have a remarkable impact on your selling and success.

There are plenty of these instruments around which try to box people and show you how to handle them differently. They are all helpful but the reason I like the Social Styles is its simplicity and power.

So where is its uniqueness? Let me explain.

The Colours – Social Styles - A Personal Profile

How can you tell what your own social style is? The following questionnaire will help you analyse your behaviour according to the four social styles. As you'll learn once you have scored your responses, some will fall into other quadrants. Remember, this profile simply highlights your most frequent tendencies.

There are no right or wrong answers in this questionnaire. This survey enables you to describe the style you use in your relationships with others.

There are twenty statements on the following pages, each followed by four different endings. For each statement, indicate the ending that best describes your behaviour in a work environment. In some cases, two choices may seem equally like you; please choose the one most like your behaviour most of the time.

When you've completed the questionnaire, score your answers according to the directions on the subsequent page.

Questions

1.   I am likely to impress others as:

    a.   practical and to the point

    b.   emotional and somewhat stimulating

    c.   supportive and dependable

    d.   intellectually orientated and rather serious

2.   In communicating with others, I may:

    a. tendency to ignore those who talk about "long-range" and direct my attention to what needs to be done right now.

    b. show impatience with ideas that show little originality.

    c. show little interest in those whose opinions are obviously not thought through and therefore risky.

    d. express frustration with those who do not have their facts straight.

3.   Sometimes, I suspect I may come across to others as being:

    a. too dominating and too intensive

    b. too emotional or too overly dramatic

    c. too agreeable or too pliable

    d. overly concerned with specifics to the point of being nit-picking

4.   When I am working on a project, I want to:

    a. work with people who want to get results quickly.

    b. work with people who are creative and interested in innovation.

    c. be stimulated and involved with people

    d. have time to gather facts and make sure the project develops systematically and logically.

5.   In any organisation, I like to:

    a. be giving orders or working independently. I don't want to waste time on "how are we going to do this". I just want to do it.

    b. give my opinions. I can take advice from people already successful in the area, not those with no "track record".

    c. work collaboratively with people, not alone. I can accept advice and direction from approving authorities.

    d. make my own decisions based on the facts at hand. I can take direction if I understand the logic behind it.

6.   When circumstances prevent me from doing what I want, I tend to:

    a. review the situation for any deficiencies on my part and take action accordingly.

    b. create a new hypothesis quickly.

    c. analyse the motivation of others and develop a fresh feel for the situation.

    d. keep in mind all the basics or history to date and pinpoint all key obstacles. I modify my plan after much thinking.

7.   When I write an email for business to someone I don't know, I usually try to:

    a. relate my purpose in writing and highlight what I want, need or expect of them.

    b. show my main points and how they work toward the future goals we both have.

    c. convey some of who I am and my style.

    d. give the background and purpose of the communication in some detail.

8.　In terms of how I think about time, I usually concentrate on:

   a.　my immediate actions and whether they work for today.

   b.　my long-range goals and how to get there. I'm not very disciplined with time.

   c.　how what I'm planning may affect other people.

   d.　ensuring the actions I take fit into the systematic program I've set up.

9.　When I meet people behaviourally, I am likely to consider whether:

   a.　they know what they're doing and can get things done.

   b.　they're exciting and creative.

   c.　friendly and open.

   d.　they seem thoughtful and reflective.

10.　When faced with people who hold a different point of view, I usually try to:

   a.　rely on my ability to pull ideas together and convince others of my ideas.

   b.　find several places we agree on to build on these and move forwards.

   c.　place me in their shoes and see their point of view.

   d.　keep my composure and help others see things logically.

11. If I were to speak before a group that didn't know me well, I would hope to leave the impression of being.

   a. a pragmatic "mover" who could assist the group in solving problems.

   b. a broad-range thinker capable of making innovative contributions.

   c. a lively person clearly in touch with the group's mood and needs, thus able to help make an impact.

   d. a systematic thinker who could help the group analyse its problems and needs.

12. In tense meetings, I occasionally:

   a. attempt to bulldoze my opinion because I'm frustrated by the process.

   b. let my hair down and express feelings better left unsaid.

   c. am swayed by others who may be solid personalities but not necessarily correct in the situation.

   d. miss the forest for the trees because I get caught in the details.

13. Sometimes, when my behaviour seems extreme, others might feel I am:

   a. dominating, brutal or harsh.

   b. moody, excitable or unpredictable.

   c. dependent, conforming or unsure.

   d. highly unemotional or detached.

14.   I feel satisfied with myself when I:

    a.   get more things accomplished than I've planned.

    b.   develop new thoughts and create ideas that can be implemented.

    c.   understand and respond in a helpful way to the feelings of others.

    d.   solve a problem using a logical method.

15.   I find I am most convincing when I can:

    a.   present options to people and help them choose an alternative.

    b.   stimulate people with new ideas and excite them into action.

    c.   be in touch with my own feelings and empathise with those of others

    d.   use logic and facts to persuade people to my point of view.

16.   When others pressure me, I am inclined to be overly:

    a.   concerned with proving myself with immediate action.

    b.   emotional and get carried away with my feelings.

    c.   concerned with what others think and tend not to take action

    d.   analytical and critical of others.

17. Under challenging situations, my approach sometimes results in being:

   a. too concerned with here and now and getting and doing what I want.

   b. so worried about settling the battle and getting to the future that I misjudge the present situation.

   c. so concerned about others that I don't think through my own situation.

   d. too involved with concepts and ideas alone.

18. I like it when others tell me they think I'm:

   a. a person who knows where they are going and is going to get there.

   b. creative and stimulating.

   c. a dependable person who comes through for them.

   d. Intellectually gifted.

19. When there's interference on a project, I usually think it's best to:

   a. concentrate on getting what I want to be accomplished right now.

   b. be original and say what I think.

   c. find out how others feel and make sure we agree on a procedure.

   d. stick to a logical, systematic, proven approach.

20. Overall, I would describe myself as:

   a. pragmatic and forceful.

   b. stimulating and creative.

   c. willing and supportive.

   d. thoughtful and industrious.

Scoring

Add up each A, B, C and D you've noted and place in the first column.

A……….. x 5 =   ……………%

B……….. x 5 =   ……………%

C……….. x 5 =   ……………%

D……….. x 5 =   ……………%

Total 20   Total 100%

Now, multiply each of your totals by 5 to determine the percentage you scored in each category and place these numbers in the second column.

For example:

A   5 x 5   = 25%

B   12 x 5 = 60%

C   3 x 5   = 15%

D   0 x 5   = 0%

Total 20   Total 100%

Interpretation

Each category, as you've probably suspected, correlates to one of the behavioural styles:

A = Red Drivers

B = Yellow Expressive

C = Blue Amiable

D = Green Analytical

In the example above, the person is primarily a yellow expressive (60%) with a strong red driver component (25%), some blue amiable (15%) and no green analytical.

The Social Styles Colours

We have the Social Style Colours. Simple to use, fun to exhibit and more importantly, extremely powerful and successful.

Integral to our understanding and use is my ABC

1. A – assess their style;

2. B – borrow their style,

3. C – communicate in their style.

To assess their style, let's look at you first to help you understand how the model works.

Social Style Colours – Assessing Your Customer

Quickly

Take a piece of paper and draw a vertical line with arrows on either end.

Now put at the top "Task and goal-focused" and at the bottom "people-focused". Gauge someone you know from work or a customer or client along this line. How goal-focused are they compared with being more concerned around people? Put an "X" where they might appear.

Next, a horizontal line cutting through the middle. On the left side, mark it "Introvert or ask," and on the right side ", extrovert or tell." Again mark an "X" where you think your person appears along the line.

"Tell" people are easy to spot – they just go around talking much of the time with few questions in their language. "Ask" people are also easy to see – they don't speak as much, and when they do, they are more interested in seeking the views of others through asking questions.

Some people like to use introvert and extravert for the exact dimensions. I like this. I'm pretty introverted, preferring to listen to people rather than talkaholic. I ask more questions to encourage this. Equally, I know extroverts who keep talking and raising the energy of groups and meetings.

Task

Introvert ← → **Extrovert**

People

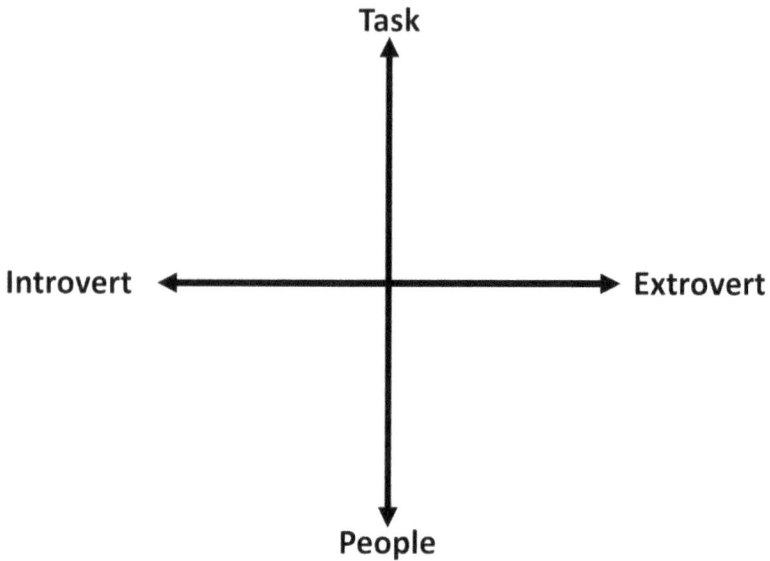

The Styles - Explained

We start to put people in these boxes from the behaviour we see from our observations.

We're not character analysing them, getting hyper psychological with this, or doing any kind of therapy; we're just figuring people and customers out a little.

I am trying to fathom what makes them tick and why. Simple, quick and easy to apply to anyone you meet.

To simplify our descriptions, I've given each box colour like this:

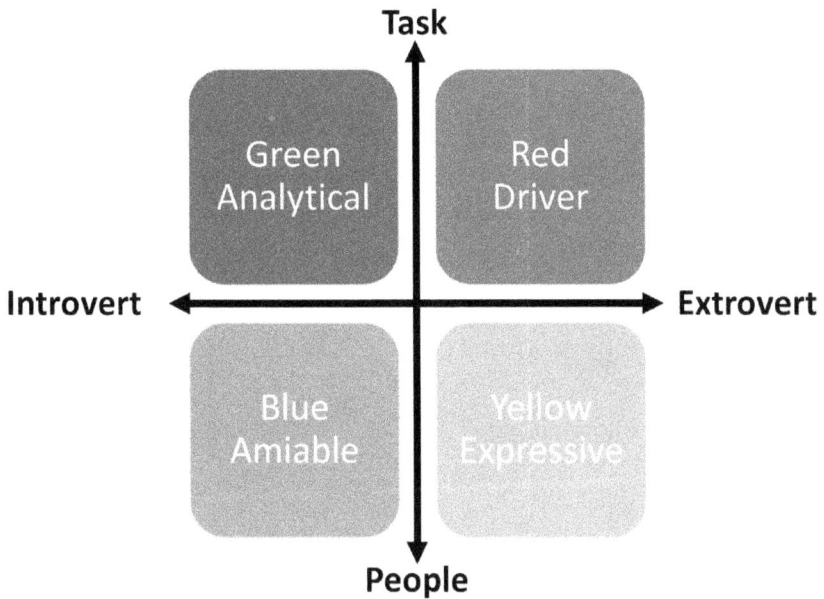

Let's describe the characteristics more and put down keywords for each colour.

Green Analytical

- Reflective
- Cautious
- Precise
- Formal
- Rules-led
- Detailed

Red Drivers

- Competitive
- Strong-willed
- Dynamic
- Decisive

- Action

Amiable Blue

- Intimate
- Caring
- Supportive
- Trusting
- Encouraging

Expressive Yellow

- Talkative
- Sociable
- Enthusiasts
- Group-oriented
- Influential
- Collaborative
- Flexible

Some Important Caveats

You can easily cross over lines and be half of one or another colour. I tend to cross over the bottom line and have some green in me plus blue, i.e., analytic and amiable, but I do have more green in me, though.

You can move quickly; we encourage that in our ABC – assess, borrow, communicate – so borrow someone else's colour and become a Smart Blue or a Smart Red. Borrowing is temporary; it's not personal and is designed to speed along the rapport and help you communicate with the customer. It smooths the wheels of communication; it is not false to who you are; this is simply a way to get on with people more, not a character analysis exercise.

I tend to use the Colours in a work setting, i.e., when I meet them in business. You can do this with a home setting if you want; it doesn't matter. You're assessing their behaviour as you see it. All it needs to be is true to them.

Oddly they might be borrowing another colour's style without even knowing they're doing so. Make sure you assess their normal behaviour. Also, care they are not in conflict with a situation or person. This changes people's behaviour to a more extreme version, so it is not helpful to use.

Recognising the Colours

Recognising Blues

Have you ever faced a large audience when about to give a stand up presentation? Maybe a business presentation, a wedding speech or an impromptu speech at the firm's Christmas party? If you have I bet you get drawn to the smilers.

It's a good tip when you're feeling a bit nervous when presenting because your audience will usually have a bunch of smilers amongst them. These people are pleasing to look at and sharing your eye contact with them does help to reduce any nerves that you might have.

Much better than imagining people in their underpants! I really don't know where that advice ever came from.

Smilers are nice people, they want you to do well and smile to encourage you. Invariably these people are blue from our colours and are usually easy to recognise.

Blue people's basic feel good factor is about caring for other people and being liked by others. They genuinely feel good when they make friends, are appreciated by other people and provide dollops of help to everyone they meet.

This gets their adrenaline flowing and makes them feel good. So look for any behaviour that shows this. Lots of smiles, eye contact, chit chat, genuine interest in you as a person, time to talk about other things other than just business. They want to get to know you as an individual.

Friendly, supportive, sincere and modest.

• Around Them	• What They Say	• How They Talk	• Body Language
• People Photos • People Items	• Tells stories, anecdotes • Shares feelings • Informal speech • Expresses opinions • Digresses	• Lots of inflection • More pitch variation • Dramatic • High volume • Fast speech	• Animated expressions • Much hand/body movement • Contact oriented • Closeness • Spontaneous actions

Recognising blue customers is not that difficult as the traits are quite easy to observe. However be careful because they may have elements of the other colours in them as well. More on this later.

Recognising Reds

Now red customers are very different to blues. Red's basic sense of worth is getting things done. Achieving things, getting results, seeing action and forward movement. Of course they have people skills like the blues but this is low down in their priorities. They get buzzed by achieving goals, being challenged, taking control, being decisive and competitive.

They don't get a kick from being nice to people and worry what others think about them. So they don't do it unless they have to.

These are not hard-nosed business people with no feelings at all. Not at all. They just put other requirements at the top of their list of wants. They get their self-worth and enjoy doing these things over and above other behaviours.

Persuasive, creative, demanding. Confident and assertive.

So how can we spot them? Vibrant reds are easy to spot as are all extremes of the colours. However most people have a lighter shade of red so are not so easy to spot.

• Around Them	• What They Say	• How They Talk	• Body Language
• Awards • Neat Piles • Power symbols • High backed chairs • Minimalism	• Tells more than asks • Talks more than listens • Lots of verbal talk • Emphatic statements • Blunt	• More vocal variety • Forceful tone • Challenging tone • Loud, fast speech	• Firm handshake • Steady eye contact • Gestures to emphasise • Displays impatience • Fast moving

Again be aware that some reds share other colours so will be slightly more difficult to spot. Also many reds know their style, and are quite proud of it, if truth be told. So they know how to mask their style to bring in more softening tones and people orientation. The issue is that they don't enjoy this, get no self-worth from this masking process…but they know they have to do it because it's expected of them. Look beyond the surface level.

Recognising Greens

Last night I was watching the late night showing of Star Trek, Next Generation. The hero from the USS Enterprise was an officer called Lieutenant Data who saved the lives of thousands of colonists by his quick detailed thinking during an attack by the Crystalline Entity.

Before you switch off, I'm not going to drone on about Star Trek but instead tell you more about Lieutenant Data.

You see Lieutenant Data is an android – a real life walking computer able to act, communicate, fight and even eat like a human being. Poor old Data, though, is devoid of personality and feelings, can be very slow as he analyses every detail in making decisions. He has a head for figures and facts and is driven by process and procedure. He can solve huge problems in his head and has a memory that houses the internet. He works alone much of the time and doesn't need human company and shows no emotion.

He's a very serious guy.

A green person's self-worth comes from achievement of structure and order. They get their kicks from autonomy, taking their time and making the right decision. Being in control, not necessarily of a team either, usually just themselves. Logical arguments and thought processes rule their lives.

Greens can be seen as calm, controlled and unemotional. This is greens seen from other perspectives. However to a green this is perfectly normal behaviour.

Caution is key, so no off-the-cuff-decisions. Principled and fair. Above all the need to be correct. These values give them a great sense of worth.

Not too difficult to spot if an extreme green, but usually people share other colours as well and will sometimes borrow other colour traits or mask their behaviour. This all makes it tricky to see.

• Around Them	• What They Say	• How They Talk	• Body Language
• Details • Systems • Charts • Organised • Functional	• Fact and task oriented • Limited sharing of feelings • More formal and proper • Focused conversation	• Little inflection • Few pitch variations • Steady, monotone delivery • Slow, soft speech	• Few facial expressions • Non-contact oriented • Few gestures

Recognising Yellows

Who's your favourite comedy impersonator?

Mike Yarwood, Harry Enfield, Paul Whitehouse...I just love the way one moment they can be impersonating a Brazilian Footballer who plays for Newcastle United and the next, a 15-year-old spotty teenager with testosterone on overdrive. Becoming the Prime Minister in one scene and then the leader of the opposition a moment later.

They have an incredible ability to change their character whilst you blink. Do you know anyone who can do this? Someone who is so flexible and changeable that you never know whether they are coming or going and don't seem to have any consistency.

By being bendable and stretchy, the yellow gets self worth. They can adopt any behaviour to suit the situation just like our comedy impersonators. Yellows love to get involved, want to be consulted, be part of a group and will bend their ways to please the group.

Flexible, adaptable and very democratic believing in everyone having their say. Good listeners and an effective compromiser if this creates group harmony.

• Around Them	• What They Say	• How They Talk	• Body Language
• Teams • Membership symbols	• Questions to gather opinions • Inconsistent • Listen more than talks • Compromise language	• Variety of tone and expression • Prefers to listen • Lots of verbal nods	• Very open • Leaning forward • Non verbal nods • Mirrors body language naturally

Recognising Colours in Online Meetings

How do we recognise the colours on video calls? Not easy as you don't have all the physical and verbal clues available when interacting in real life. However:

- Reds will appear more impatient and will want a schedule. Will start on time and expect you to finish on time too. Their backgrounds may be plain or unimportant. Possibly a shelf with various awards and trappings, but that's too stereotypical, even for reds. They may have advertising or company banners behind them. They will be well lit and have the right equipment to operate from. Eye contact will be intense; their video will be on but probably muted to start with. Anything to speed the meeting along.

- Greens will have a minimal unclutter background. Possibly a bookshelf. They may have their video switched off until reminded to show the screen. Ultimately they would have preferred email. They will know the software in meticulous detail, so maybe a little slow to adopt it.

- Yellows will be talkative. Their mics will be on all the time, interacting with others and wanting to chat to break the ice early. Their backgrounds will be well thought through. Colourful, stylish and curated perfectly.

- Blues will be the quietest of them all. Mics off to start with and video on when reminded. They will want to start slowly and carefully. Naturally, they will yearn for the return of onsite meetings. They may show family items in their background, and their pets appear.

These are all very stereotyped but helpful recognition factors.

Here are some tips to add to your repertoire when handling the colours online:

- Reds thrive in competition and being heard, so give them the opportunity with quizzes and breakout rooms where they can talk to others. You'll find reds will volunteer to lead.

- Greens will relish some preparation opportunities to get it right the first time. Furnish them with whatever they need to prepare thoroughly.

- Yellows will want to socialise. Perhaps before the due start time, set up a meet and greet breakout room where they and like-minded souls can chat before the meetings start. Interaction and collaboration are vital for yellows.

- Blues will want time to connect with others, eye contact and seeing people is essential. They want to build a rapport in their own time, so forced networking of 5 minutes may be off-putting for them.

Again, this serves as being helpful, not a certainty.

Influencing Each Colour

We've done the A; now we're doing the B and C – the borrowing and communicating in their style. What are the dos and don'ts?

Look at this comprehensive list and see if you recognise any traits of people you know.

Influencing Green Analytical

- Provide facts and data in a logical, organised format.
- Don't be disorganised or messy.
- Approach them in a straightforward, direct way.
- Stick to business.
- Don't joke, be casual, informal or loud.
- Support their principles.
- Use a thoughtful approach to build your credibility by listing the pros and cons of any suggestions you make.
- Don't rush the decision-making process.
- Contribute to their efforts.
- Present specifics, and do what you say you can do.
- Don't be vague about what is expected of either of you.
- Do not fail to follow through.
- Take your time, but be persistent.
- Don't waste time.
- Draw up a scheduled approach to delivery; assure them there will be no surprises.
- Don't leave things to chance or luck. If you agree, follow through.
- Don't threaten, persuade or coax.

- If you disagree, make an organised presentation of your position.

- Don't use testimonies of others or unreliable sources. Give them time to verify the reliability of your actions.

- Be accurate and realistic.

- Don't use other people's opinions as evidence.

- Provide solid, tangible, practical evidence.

- Don't use gimmicks or clever manipulators.

- Give them time to be thorough.

- Don't push too hard or be unrealistic with deadlines.

Influencing Red Drivers

- Be clear, specific, brief and to the point.

- Don't ramble on or waste their time.

- Stick to business.

- Don't try to build a personal relationship.

- Come prepared with all their requirements in a well organised "package".

- Don't be disorganised or messy.

- Do not confuse or distract their mind from the business.

- Present the facts logically and concisely.

- Don't leave loopholes or vague issues.

- Ask specific (preferably "what") questions

- Don't ask rhetorical or irrelevant questions.

- Provide alternatives and choices for them to make their own decisions.

- Don't come with a ready-made decision, and do not decide for them.

- Provide facts and figures about the probability of success of effectiveness of options

- Don't speculate wildly or offer guarantees and assurances if you can't be sure.

- If you disagree, take issues with facts, not the person.

- If you disagree, do not let it reflect on them personally.

- If you agree, support the results, not the person.

- Motivate and persuade by referring to objectives and results.

- Don't try to convince by "personal means."

- Support their conclusions.

- Don't direct or order

- After finishing business, leave quickly.

- Don't stay for a personal chat after business.

Influencing Blue Amiables

- Start with a personal comment; break the ice.

- Don't rush into business or the schedule.

- Show interest in them as people, find areas of common interest, and be candid and open.

- On the other hand, don't stick solely to business; on the other hand, do not lose sight of goals by being too personal.

- Draw out personal objectives and work to help achieve these.

- Listen and be responsive.

- Don't force them to respond to your objectives; do not say, "This is how I see the situation."

- Present your case softly, in a non-threatening manner.

- Don't be overbearing or demanding; do not threaten them with a position of power.

- Ask "how" questions to draw out their opinions.

- Don't debate about facts and figures.

- Observe for possible areas of early disagreement or dissatisfaction.

- Don't manipulate or bully them into agreeing because they probably will not fight back.

- If you disagree, look for hurt feelings and changes in attitude.

- Behave casually and informally.

- Don't be abrupt and rapid.

- Define clearly, preferably in writing, individual contributions.

- Don't be vague.

- Do not offer options and probabilities.

- Reassure that their decision will minimise risks and emphasise the benefits.

- Don't offer assurances and guarantees you cannot fulfil.

- Provide personal assurances.

- Give clear, specific solutions with maximum guarantees.

Influencing Yellow Expressives

- Support their dreams and intuitions.

- Don't lay down the law or suppress their opinions.

- Don't be dogmatic.

- Leave time for socialising.

- Don't be curt, cold or tight-lipped.

- Talk about people and their objectives; they find opinions stimulating.

- Don't concentrate on facts and figures, alternatives, abstractions, or detail.

- Get their commitment to a course of action.

- Don't leave decisions up in the air.

- Ask for their opinions and ideas about people.

- Don't waste time trying to be impersonal, business-like, task-orientated.

- Provide ideas for carrying out decisions.

- Control "dreaming" with them, or you will lose time.

- Use enough time to be stimulating, fun-loving, fast-moving.

- Don't mess around too much; don't stick too rigidly to the plan either.

- Don't talk down to them; do not patronise.

Social Style Needs Summary

	Green	Blue	Red	Yellow
Primary Asset	Systematic	Supportive	Focused	Energising
Back-up Behaviour	Avoid	Acquiesce	Autocratic	Attack
For Growth Needs to	Decide	Initiate	Listen	Check
Strongest Personal Motivator	Respect	Approval	Results	Recognition
Needs Climate That	Describes	Supports	Commits	Collaborates
Let Them Save	Face	Relationships	Time	Effort
Try to be	Accurate	Agreeable	Efficient	Stimulating
Support Their	Principles and thinking	Relationships and feelings	Conclusions and actions	Visions and intuitions
For Decisions Give Them	Data and evidence	Assurances and guarantees	Options and probabilities	Testimony and incentives
Follow up with	Service	Support	Action	Attention

Selling with Social Style Colours

The Social Styles Colours is a brilliant tool to help salespeople recognise the motivations and drivers of customers as they get to know them. It's quick to understand, relatively accurate, and something that can be used throughout the sales process.

In essence, within a couple of minutes, you can gauge how the customer "ticks". Very useful.

- Blue people are motivated by people

- Red is driven by performance

- Green is motivated by the process

- Yellows love a bit of flexibility and social

Here are lots of ideas to help you when you've recognised the customer's colour under each element of the four-stage sales process:

1. Initiate Relationship

2. Explore Needs

3. Suggest a Course of Action

4. Obtain Agreement

Initiate Relationship

Blue

- Build relationship before business
- Match vigorously
- Ask for thoughts and feelings
- Explore family

Red

- Be confident
- Take control
- Show conviction and belief
- Move the process forward

Green

- Draw up an agenda
- Show you've prepared and researched
- Be to the point

Yellow

- Involve the partner more
- Talk about the family
- Show flexibility to the sales process

Explore Needs

Blue

- Explore very softly
- Sugar your questions
- Listen intently
- Summarise regularly

Red

- Keep it short and business like
- Listen to their strategy
- Recognise their achievements

Green

- Keep away from soft facts too much
- Focus on hard facts
- Use and share a structure to your questions
- Ask them to pre-prepare some answers

Yellow

- Ask about other people involved with their plans
- Freewheel with your questioning
- Let them talk, they will

Suggest a Course of Action

Blue

- Emphasise loyalty you'll have with them
- Personalise the solution

Red

- Move quickly and show how speedily you can move
- Summarise the key benefits and facts
- Show how the solution achieves their goal

Green

- Logical presentation with all the facts
- Eliminate risks
- Specifics
- Well researched, show your research

Yellow

- Present some options or some choices within the solution
- Emphasise the tailoring on the approach to their needs
- Show how their "collective" will benefit
- Involve the other people in the solution

Obtain Agreement

Blue

- Ask how they feel about the solution "How do you feel?"
- Show how you'll maintain contact

Red

- Show how quickly you can get the ball rolling
- Ask "shall we get moving them"
- Ask them "does this achieve your goals?"
- Be prepared, they may test you with some challenges. Meet them head on

Green

- Emphasise efficiency in the solution
- Ask them "does it feel logical"

Yellow

- Ask them "which option do you want to go ahead with?"

Summary and Actions

- Assess yourself and know why

- Colour your customers when you meet them, add their colour to your CRM system so you can quickly recall their colour

- Use the ABC without remorse

- Learn a few do's and don't for each colour when handling your customers. Try to borrow a couple of additional traits every time but return them when done.

- Be true to who you are. You are only "borrowing" their behaviours and ways to accentuate the communication between yourselves. If your intentions are sound, ethical and moral, then you are in the clear.

- Make sure you access people's colours and yours when there is harmony and good nature. A sniff of conflict, anger or confrontation and people's manners and ways change. So not to be relied upon.

- Remember that no one colour is better than any other.

- I have primarily green in me, with tinges of blue. Yes, you can cross over the line.

Now We Can Lead

WIIFM

WIIFM Broadcasting. No it's not an American Radio Station broadcasting out of Los Angeles. It's something all customers ask themselves when you ask something of them. It's also a motto for the Gen Y's Generation – these guys are coming of age now, and are potential customers.

WIIFM should be the guiding principle for every customer interaction we do. Let me tell you more.

This morning I received a charming letter from an oil company in Hereford asking if I would fill out some personal details so they could update their database. I bought a tank of household oil from them a couple of months ago.

They wanted email addresses, phone numbers etc. They even put in a pre-paid envelope. Decent of them.

I thought to myself…I have a list of jobs to do this Saturday morning or I can fill in this form, so WIIFM – what's in it for me?

There was nothing in it for me to fill in the form. I have no loyalty to them as I use an oil aggregator service on the internet called Boiler Juice who source the most competitive oil from the market when I need it.

I thought if only she had given me a good reason to fill in the details such as:

- We can keep you informed of our special offers.

- We can let you know when we're delivering in your area and can fill up your tank for you with no delivery charge.

- A prize draw for a bottle of champagne or a hamper or a free 500 litres delivery of oil. Now we're talking.

- If there was something in it for me, then I would have filled in the form.

So remember WIIFM. Every time you contact your customer, and this includes all those internal ones inside your company, get into their shoes and try and figure out what's in it for them. Make sure you vocalise this. This works for managing people as well, persuasion, influencing, delegating.

And if they're a Gen Y, you'll see the words WIIFM tattooed on the back of their neck. Go on and check the next teenager or early twenties person. You'll be amazed how much this matters to them.

So where did the letter end up? It was going in the bin, until I saw it was signed personally by Denise, who is probably just following direction from above. Shame on you from above, tell Denise about WIIFM. Remember nowadays everyone has sales in their job description, even if it's not in their title.

Always Give a Reason

We use a Print on Demand company to manage sales of a variety of books that we sell. It works very well. On the odd occasion, misprinting occurs and my customers feed this back to me very quickly, and I send out a new copy immediately. The last time this happened I asked them if they would refund the cost of an item that had been printed upside down. The cost price was £6.50. They asked me to send in a photo of the upside-down book.

For £6.50 I couldn't be bothered and told them so and that they really ought to trust me after all we have completed hundreds of pounds of business with them.

Expecting nothing in response, I received an email from a superior.

She gave a reason, i.e. "so we can show the printers in order for them to not repeat the mistake".

This changed everything. I realised why they wanted the photo. It wasn't because they didn't trust me, which I thought, it was to improve their service.

I contacted my customer who sent through a photo which I forwarded on and £6.50 was refunded.

If only the first person had given a reason then it would have ended amicably a whole lot sooner.

So whenever you make any request always give a reason and you'll be amazed as to the response, it all makes sense really.

If you want to influence or persuade someone tell them because; because works hypnotically. And I didn't even tell you the photocopier story.

Pull or Push

Influencing behaviours can be conveniently spit into pull or push and this helps us to determine which style we may have used in the past and which we would want to use more of in the future.

Pull influencing involves motivating people, using your personality to its full effect to pull people towards your viewpoint, using benefits to help solve problems and issues. In other words, dragging the customer to your goal that also satisfies their goals as well.

Success factors to be able to use pull influencing techniques involve:

- The quality of the questions used to obtain information and check understanding.

- The ability to put yourself in the customer's shoes.

- The skill to build on your customer's proposals.

- The ability to forge relationships and coalitions to influence people.

As we can see these are classic consultancy selling skills, problem solving and objective achieving.

Pull influencing can bring extensive results often culminating in a long term relationship and a trusted adviser status being achieved. But both pull and push have their place.

Push influencing is the opposite and uses your skills to persuade and move the customer to the position of change which brings about a win-win relationship. Using logical arguments and facts to persuade, bargaining and negotiating, using punishment or rewards to coerce the customer or authority to move them.

Some of these will blatantly not work in a sales situation but are used by others to influence, particularly in management and team situations. However, many traditional influencers will attempt to persuade by extolling the virtues and benefits of their products or services by using logical arguments, benefits and will overcome objections at the drop of a hat to push the customer towards a decision.

Success factors for push-based influencing come down to:

- The quality of your ideas and reasoning

- Your credibility and authority

- Your ability to get the right people to support your proposal

Push based influencing has its place but is not as effective as pull-based influencing. The reason is that power forms the basis of much of the pull influencing. And power can be too forceful in sales.

The use of power in influencing has been used successfully for centuries. Let's have a look at how power can be used in B2B influencing situations.

Power can be divided up neatly:

- Personal power – your personality, magnetism, gift of the gab. Many influencers drown the customer in their charisma attempting to be liked and this can be effective pull behaviour but won't work with every customer and is quite an old fashioned approach.

- Positional power – your rank, position in the organisation, who you know. For example, your sales director may gain access to your customer, whereas the foot soldier would be turned away by your customer's PA.

- Expert power – your knowledge of your product and industry, being a specialist in the field, being logical in your approach. This power can influence considerably but can be overdone by subject matter experts who like to soak the customer in the features and aspects of their product. Using expertise to push the customer to your goal can be overbearing.

- Coercive power – exerting pressure to force a decision, deadlines, buy now whilst stocks last. Buyers see right through this technique nowadays. Coercive power is essentially the stick. Something we use with our children to influence or persuade. Not appropriate in a sales situation.

- Reward power – the opposite of coercive power where the use of rewards can still bring about decisions but have to be used carefully in the modern economy. Corporate hospitality, gifts come to mind here. However rewards such as additional help and advice, your expertise on tap, support from your colleagues within your organisation, information, marketing assistance are much more subtle and are the currency of a trusted adviser.

The Body Language of Influencing in public

Next time you watch a politician on TV speaking to an audience, turn the volume down and watch. Then interpret what is being said just by observing the body language. Try it – it's amazing what you read into the message just by watching the person speaking.

How many of you have made your mind up about a speaker's message without concerning yourself about the words, purely by observation and your intuition? And this is going on right now somewhere in the world. A business speaker has a good message but it's being clouded by the way it's presented.

The purpose of this book is to remind you, no, convince you of some key steps to take to ensure your body doesn't cloud the message next time you get up and speak.

Let's kick off with the body language and work around the body reminding ourselves of what to do. We'll then cover movement around your stage.

The Head

My daughter had just started playgroup and she brought home a picture of Daddy. An amazing picture showing Daddy with a large smiling face and 2 arms and legs. However, the body was missing. This happened with my sons when they first went to playgroup.

DADDY
18TH Feb 2005

Inquisitive as ever, I asked the nursery teacher why Bethan had missed out on the body. "Children of that age don't focus on the body, they are only concerned with the face and that's all they see. That's why clowns paint their faces so brightly and children love them".

As adults, we still have childish habits and one of them is to focus on the face of someone who is speaking to you. So get those expressions working for you and really exaggerate the meaning. Smile, frown, look angry, shocked, amazed – but please always be congruent with your message.

Eye Contact

Next, we have eye contact. This is probably the one skill, when mastered, that does the most to engage the audience and build trust and rapport with the audience. The rule is to hardly ever let go. Imagine you're playing tennis or squash. You never let your eye off the ball otherwise you'll miss a shot. Likewise, keep your eye contact on the audience at all times.

Careful with the lighthouse technique as well – this is where speakers sweep the audience in a repetitive swishing motion that does more to put people to sleep than engage.

It always reminds me of those old Second World War POW escape movies when the escapees are nudging their way out of the tunnel dodging the sweeping searchlights. As soon as the light has moved along its repetitive motion, they dash to safety. In a similar way your audience will escape you when your sweeping leaves them.

Instead have a conversation with your audience with your eyes. Randomly contact with each audience member and give them 2 to 3 seconds of eye contact and move onto the next person. Maintain this random movement. Find those in the audience who like just a little more eye contact and be aware of those who want slightly less.

When faced with a large audience – I mean more than 25 or so people, adopt a similar habit but don't give each person eye contact. That'll take ages. Instead, clump people into small groups and give these clumps the same eye contact as if they were one person. I tell you, that because of the distance between you and a large audience this gives people the impression that you are looking at them.

Feet

Now let's go to the other extreme of your body. Your feet and legs. Now what do you do with these limbs. Not a lot really, unless you are moving around your stage, that's a movement with a purpose, not aimless wandering that only distracts the audience.

Do you remember your mother asking you to stand up straight? Maybe it really was good advice. Try to stand with both feet firmly on the ground, pretty much the same distance apart as your shoulders. Keep them balanced so your body is not leaning to one side. Don't look like a catwalk model or if you're supping a pint at the bar of your local. Stand straight and look professional, not a slouch.

Nerves…that's a word than conjures up fear and dread every time people stand up and speak in public. And sure enough you'll have nerves. Professionals call it adrenaline and you need that to do a really good job. If you don't have nerves or adrenaline, you might as well not bother because you can't be bothered. So welcome nerves, call them adrenaline and make them work for you.

Nerves will show in the periphery of your body. The ends such as feet, hands, head. Keeping your feet still transfers this energy to the top part of your body where it should go.

Now I didn't say you should stay rigid to the spot; that would be terrible for 20 minutes. Instead focus your attention on preventing aimless movement, pacing up and down, shifting from side to side. Keep well balanced and professional.

The Body

Next we have the trunk. That's the bit my daughter missed out. Not much you can do with the trunk apart from keeping it straight. Not like the Sergeant Major on the parade ground but not slouched either. Relaxed and comfortable. The worst sin is to block the invisible midline that runs from between your 2 feet and your head. Block it and you place a barrier with your audience. Just don't block it – that's the rule.

Hands and Arms

Next the arms and hands. I've spoken with hundreds of people who honestly don't know what to do with their hands.

Shame really, so they copy people on the TV, especially weather girls. They grasp their hands together. I've never understood this although I was guilty myself once. It made me feel better and comfortable so much that as soon as I stood up to talk, my two hands came together. And when I got really nervous, I used to rub them together too. Someone told me I looked like a market trader making lots of money. That sure went down well with my audiences.

So what do you do with them? Behind your backs but that just reminds me of Prince Charles. In your pockets I hear you say. No, you're hiding something, keeping back from the audience and besides, you're missing out on a great weapon. No, the answer is to use them to back up your message by gesturing.

I did some training work in the Netherlands earlier this year for an international food company. The delegates were from all over Europe – Spain, Italy, Germany, Netherlands, France…I watched each one present on many occasions and it was so great to watch those from Mediterranean countries who naturally speak with their hands. They gesture so well and when given the go-ahead to gesture during their speeches, they really went for it. Us Anglo Saxons are the stilted ones and need to learn to speak with our hands.

One of my dying wishes was to go to Glastonbury and in 2004, I finally bought the tickets. I hired a camper van for the weekend, I still like some creature comforts. When I'm watching the bands playing on stage, I imagine that the gestures of the lead singer will be dramatic. If he wants us to clap, he won't politely pat his hands together, he'll launch them over his head to make a very dramatic clap.

This is how we should gesture with audiences. Large dramatic gestures to help the audience understand what you're saying. Broad gestures that welcome every person into your speech, building rapport. Think of your speech content and let your hands do the talking. Watch deaf people doing their sign language – it really is a very clever way of finding your gesture buttons.

And when not gesturing, or talking, maybe standing still to take questions from your audience, assume the assertive stance. Standing straight with your arms and hands down your sides in a relaxed assertive and confident manner.

Body Movement

Finally, body movement. Movement can be an enormously effective way of engaging the audience into your message. Clean your stage – remove obstacles, tape wires to the floor, so you don't trip over them, place the screen to the side.

Yes, to the side, and I wish more meeting planners would situate their screen to the right or left of the audience and not bang in the middle. You've probably been there or seen it. The slides are beaming onto the screen, the table is full of people, so to let the person on your left see the screen, you move into the corner of the room. You're lost, you're gone – you've lost eye contact with the audience who are busy reading the slides.

If you're able to position the screen to the left or right of the audience, you'll be able to remain in the centre of the stage. Trust what is on your slides and be aware of reading directly from the screen – this takes your eye contact away from the audience and is a cardinal sin. Have a laptop screen in front of you or learn your slides. Better still use fewer of them but that's another story.

Once you have a clear space do move around with a purpose. I've used past, present and future by gradually moving along an imaginary line. The audience can see the time moving along as well as hear. I've used one side of the stage for showing the advantages of an idea I'm promoting and the other side, the disadvantages. I've placed flipcharts at both sides of the room to mirror these place anchors.

Move forward towards your audience when you want to make a really big point. Move backwards when you want them to reflect on something. Move to your left or right to change the subject or pace of your delivery.

Do move around your stage but with a distinct purpose.

The next time you're observing and listening to a speaker, try and cut out the sound and focus entirely on the visual aspects. Try and interpret what he or she is saying just by the body language alone. You may not be right in your assumption of the meaning, but it's the impression that everyone else is probably getting too. And first impressions last for ages.

A Touching Way of Getting Agreement

Researchers operating in an American shopping mall demonstrated that a touch on the customer's upper arm for about half a second had a miraculous result.

- 63% of those shoppers touched, shopped for more.

- 23% of those shoppers touched, spent more money.

Wow!

So the tip here is to lightly touch your customer's upper arm just before you want them to take some action, buy your product, refer you on to someone else in the organisation, or sign the contract.

Chances are it'll increase your closing rates and help you influence your customer more.

Try it…go on…take a risk.

Signpost Your Way to A Close

How did a visit to an ancient castle outdo a 21st Century experiential science museum with some of the best attractions ever invented?

Simple – the ancient castle was a better visitor attraction because they had learnt a vital lesson which we can use in influencing.

I took a week off last month with my family and we decided to go and visit some attractions for a few days. I remember two places we visited and enjoyed as being completely the opposite to each other. How were they so different?

One attraction let us loose in the place and the other carefully guided us along a pre-ordained path to enjoy ourselves.

And which one did we enjoy the most?

So where's the moral here for influencing? Simple really. When influencing a customer or presenting to an audience, you must take them along a path and explain what that path is and mention when you get to certain points in the journey.

Tell them that you'll want to show them how the product might help them a little later on and they can make some decisions if they wish to. Explain where you are in the process and what you want to do next.

The day out we enjoyed the most was Sudeley Castle in Gloucestershire. As soon as we stepped out of the entrance we were guided with signs and posters where to go. At every junction we could see a map illustrating where our adventure was going next and I could see that I was going to enjoy all the sites the castle had to offer. Brilliant.

The other place, an experiential science museum in Bristol, just let us loose as soon as we left the payment counter. I was faced with a myriad of decisions and options to choose and I didn't know where to start.

So adopt a signposting culture the next time you're with clients or presenting to a group of people and you'll give them the best experience possible.

5 James Bond Style Influencing Tips

My name is Bond…James Bond. I Just love that opening from Sean Connery who is the James Bond I remember from my youth. And wasn't he just so smooth and such a debonair character? Here are 5 body language tips used by James Bond and others to create a great impression and to really influence people.

1. James Bond always stood well. An assertive stance that was enough to fend off his enemies and charm the women. He did this simply by standing with a balanced centre of gravity. He didn't sway from one side to the other or lean on one leg, he stood still, assertively and balanced. Try it next time, it's hard to change a habit of a lifetime but if you want to stand like James Bond, well…

2. James Bond would have a variety of facial expressions to create a mood or cause a stir but his most powerful was his smile. If you looked close enough you could see his secret. He broke into a smile but he did it slowly. I mean sloooowly. You see, a face breaking into a smile can be encouraging, but if done too quickly, we see through this as a fraud and distrust the person. But if done slowly, it comes over as genuine and a smile we warm to.

3. Breathing was another strategy used by James Bond. Of course it was I hear you say, otherwise, he'd die. Bond's breathing was deep and diaphragmatic from the stomach and this gave a confident and assertive impression. Breathing high and quick can mean nervousness, unsteadiness and unconfident. Not an impression James Bond wanted to make as 007 secret agent.

4. James was an expert at positive strokes, in other words making people feel good with his compliments. But the way he did this was very clever. He'd plan his sentence such as "You're looking particularly attractive today Miss Moneypenny", and he'd physically deliver the compliment with his hands. As he began the sentence, his arms would be outstretched pointing to the person and at the moment he uttered the key word, which in our example is attractive, he'd unravel his fingers to point directly at the person just as though he was giving them the key compliment. Very suave. So stretch out your arms, leaving your elbows at your waist as you deliver the compliment and at the key word unravel your fingers so you point at the person. Real cool.

5. Finally, and I'm leaving the best to last. If you want to sound as confident as James Bond, imitate the way he said his name and watch his head. He'd say, "My name is Bond, James Bond", but not in a monotone way. Instead, he would drop his head so his voice fell dramatically at the second Bond. This caused a sensation of confidence and assuredness that no one could match and both men and women melted…as he intended.

Next time you say your name, practice the James Bond head drop, it really works and is fun too.

What's Your Audience's Bone?

Here's a technique to get your audience's attention quickly and succinctly when you're running a seminar or workshop.

What do you do to get a dog's attention?

You give them a treat, a bone maybe.

Then they're all yours.

Likewise find out what your audience's bone is. It may be to learn some new sales techniques to make even more money. It could be to learn some new ideas to keep them ahead of the competition. It's possibly to help them manage their sales team better.

Find out and then throw the bone out right up front. That's right. Ignore the seminar agenda, the obligatory objectives slide and the boring delegate introductions.

Just give them the bones up front and you'll have their attention for the next part.

Reward Don't Punish

Over Christmas, I visited my father in France and hired a car to get around. On my first trip to the gym in the nearby town, I drove down a side street which was clearly restricted to 30 MPH (about 45 KPH local).

Now back in the UK, I would have been scolded for creeping above 30, with an automated sign telling me to slow down you bad person. Perhaps an angry resident with a mock speed camera or at the very least a massive sign telling me the speed limit and to slow down or else.

In France, it was refreshingly different.

An LED-lit sign with a smiley face when I was below 30 and an unhappy sad face when I creeped above.

An immediate impact, you are rewarded, which brings pleasure and reassurance.

So, in sales management, in business, try to reward more than scold. Reward is more superior than punishment, just ask the French.

The Perils of But

The one word in the English language with the most detrimental effect is "but". The word "but" puts too much emphasis on what follows. It has its purpose but we use it incorrectly.

Your intention was sound but….

Here comes the put down, the critique.

We know this instinctively; we hold our breath ready for the next sentence. Our defences engage and we prepare for an equal response.

The trick is to remove the "but" and replace with "and". This disarms the receiver for the remainder of the sentence and allows a neutral delivery.

So, next time you hear yourself using "but", stop, pause and replace with "and" you'll be amazed as to the response.

However, there is a place for "but".

But there's more

- Use "want to" instead of "have to"
- Use "won't" instead of "can't"
- Use "I'd like to" instead of "I'm afraid to".

Catch you later, but have a great one first. But if you don't it's your volition.

Use Speed Bumps in Emails to Ensure They're Read

How can road speed reduction methods help your customer to read the whole email you sent them? Here's how, let me explain.

In towns and cities, 30 mph limited roads are strewn with speed bumps. These annoy motorists, and damage cars but do slow traffic right down. They work.

Emails are a problem just like roads in town. People speed through them both. Speed bumps slow cars down so speed bumps can also slow people down reading emails to ensure they get the whole message.

How can you add speed bumps to an email? Here's some ideas

- Write smaller sentences
- Have shorter paragraphs
- Aim to have just one topic covered
- Have odd headings to stimulate
- Change font and size to stop the reader in their track
- Colour the important paragraph

- Use "urgent", "don't skip this bit" as paragraph breaks

Try one or two next time you send an important email and you'll be amazed how much attention people will give to the contents.

Snow and Hot Buttons

Last week we had colossal dollops of snow hit our tiny island, something we're not used to, or can cope with. People say it's the coldest winter since 1963 here in the UK. Let me explain how a freezing winter can help you really clarify your customer's needs whilst influencing your product or idea.

As a result, everything ground to a halt – schools closed, the road system jammed, businesses sent workers home and gas supplies had to be imported from Norway to cope with the central heating demand.

But we all had a whale of a time. Euan was outside as soon as it was daylight sledging and playing snowballs with his friends, Lewis thought it would be extra time on Xbox Live with his Xbox Crew, Bethan wanted to phone her girlfriends to say how wonderful it was, and me…

…I was glad to be at home that day and praying that the broadband and electricity stayed on and I could contact my clients.

You see, snow means diverse things to different people and when we're influencing things, products, services or ideas, we need to appreciate that our customers see things differently and like varying aspects of whatever we're influencing. Just because we think our widget is great for this or that doesn't mean that our customer thinks the same.

Customers have "hot buttons" which they attach to things they buy. The five global hot buttons are security, convenience, power, comfort and peace.

When they apply these hot buttons to our product/idea/service it's called their buying criteria and it helps us to see what they want from our product.

For example, I'm really into convenience, I guess I'm quite lazy, so I need products to help me save time and effort and make things easy for me. So when I bought my VW Golf a couple of years ago, knowing that the service interval was 25,000 miles really ticked my box.

A customer might be into power, so you show how your car can make them look good in their neighbourhood, stroke their ego a little.

Your client is into comfort so knowing that your investment product has built in professional discretionary management, might float their boat.

Now my wife gets me to do DIY around the house by threatening to call a man who can do the job. She knows that my pride will certainly make me do the job – my power hot button.

So next time you're with your customer, ask them about the pain you're solving and what it means to them personally, to find out their buying criteria. "What are you looking for in…?" is a great question to ask.

And is it the coldest winter since 1963? I don't know yet, it's still going on, but what I do know is if it wasn't for the cold winter of 1963, I wouldn't be here now. Apparently it was so cold without central heating, people had to go to bed. Now there's some buying criteria for you. :-)

Get Put Through by Sounding Important

I'm sure you're making more prospecting calls at the moment, just like everyone else, so I'm guessing that you're coming across barriers in getting to talk to your prospective customers. If that barrier is a Personal Assistant who's trained to stop you in your tracks, here's a neat little tip that just might get you put through.

A UCLA survey showed that on the telephone a massive 84% of the message and meaning is derived purely from your voice. This is a well known fact and was substantiated by Albert Mehrabian in the 1970s.

I'm suggesting that you sound important so you can get through the gatekeeper.

Important people have deeper voices and say things in shorter sentences. Their tone of voice falls at the end of each sentence to accentuate their importance and they leave lots of pauses.

And most people when faced with someone who sounds ever so important will put you through without hesitation. Try it, it works and is also fun.

How to Get Immediate Attention

I'm on an express train travelling home from Glasgow. The Virgin Pendolino is whizzing at over 100mph through the Scottish Borders and the ride is relaxed. The problem is, we started 15 minutes late, and I've a connection at Lancaster, which I'm going to miss.

On the intercom, an announcement begins "I've just found out that this train has caught up and is now on schedule". I breathed a sigh of relief.

The announcement piqued my attention, funny that. But using the phrases:

- Breaking news

- I've got good news

- We've recently developed a new service

- I've just discovered

Will pique people's interest and gain enough attention to continue with your sales message.

Useful? Try it when you're next making a call, or starting a presentation or looking to get an audience's attention. It works.

How to Command Attention

On holiday last year in Porthleven, Cornwall, storms had ravaged the coastline overnight. The following morning I stumbled across this sign warning of the perils of swimming today.

It stopped me in my tracks as it appealed to every sense of survival embedded in me. However, it felt wrong, the words of an exasperated person.

In selling, this tactic has often been used to persuade customers to buy. Project Fear was its name during Brexit and when done badly, has a detrimental effect on the customer, driving them away.

We call this "Away From" motivation and it's known that a fair proportion of people and businesses buy things on fear of loss or to prevent problems escalating. You know, the training manager hiring extra training to avoid a fine by their regulator.

On saying that, it's also well documented that people buy things to gain pleasure or to achieve some goal or objective. "Towards" motivation. For example, I'm developing live internet streaming from my studio here and wanted a first-class camera and steaming encoding software. Vimeo came along, and I bought their solution to help me achieve this goal.

My experience says that away it varies from customer to customer and context around it. You have to ask them early – "What drove you to see me?" or "What's important about this to you?"

In the case, of a life or death scenario on a beautiful beach in Cornwall, perhaps the fear tactic was the best one to use.

How Do You Demonstrate Your Capability?

Watching over the UK's skies is a brand new jet fighter called the Typhoon flown by expert pilots to ward off baddy planes from other countries. Recently I saw a video clip of one such incursion from a Long-Range Russian Bomber. The Typhoon flew alongside and then flipped sideways to show the Russian crew the various weapons it had tied to its undercarriage.

It's here on YouTube https://youtu.be/Nf05A8BhuqY

This was enough evidence of the firepower to ward them off, and the Russian Bear flew off in the other direction.

The same is true in sales. We don't have to arrive with our six-shooters ready in our holsters like a Wild West cowboy, but we do need to demonstrate our credibility to build trust and a relationship.

Some ideas:

- Write and publish a book (I have 9)
- Publish plenty of content online showing your expertise and credibility
- Speak at industry events
- Build your reputation and brand
- Dress the part – remember the 90:90 rule
- Refine your communication skills

The list can go on, but don't put all your weapons inside your jacket and flash them; only a fully armed Typhoon can do that — what a sight and what a job is flying one of those.

Help Them Visualise Using It

Last night I was watching a programme on the TV which involved a young couple who had to make a big choice when it came to buying a new home.

One home was on the French Atlantic coastline, a beautiful stretch of land glistening in the warmth of the sunshine. The house was fantastic, 4 bedrooms, sun terrace and full of original features….

The other place was in Exmouth in Devon, equally sublime but didn't share the same climate. It was a two-bedroom terraced Victorian house with a garden overlooked by plenty of others.

Two estate agents covered each region and you would have thought the French one would have won hands down because of the location and property. But no, the Exmouth agent just had a knack of presenting his property better.

He continually helped the couple to imagine what it would be like living there, what they would use the garden for, who they would invite to the barbeques, when would they nip down to the sea, where would they fit their furniture…and so on.

Once they'd had the tour of the property in Exmouth, they could see themselves living there.

Now the poor agent in France did none of this. She pointed out good features but just kept on talking and talking and talking. And then more talking.

You can guess which one they chose.

So think about how you present your product or solution and help your customer to own it. Help them to visualise how they would use it.

If you sell insurance, before you do any questioning strings, help them visualise what it's like to be in a wheelchair or to be too weak to climb the stairs let alone get back to work to earn some money. Help them see this, smell it, experience it in their mind's eye.

If you sell real estate, help them see what it'll be like to live there, imagine their new lifestyle.

If you sell big TVs, help them imagine what it would be like to sit on the sofa watching England beat Brazil in the final.

Don't tell them, help them to visualise it. Use questions to steer their thinking and imagination.

England 2 – Brazil 1. Now that's something rather delicious to visualise.

Why Trust is Sooo Important Right Now

Last night I was having a healthy supper and an equally healthy debate about the trials and tribulations of working from home. We both agreed that being based at home was no longer an issue, and if your work involves a laptop, your brain and cloud data; then you can work anywhere.

The real debate started over Zoom Video calls or phone calls to prospects and customers. Shelley's response and she happens to be a fan of the phone, was "they don't need to see me, I have a big brand behind me."

And it's true. Her company dominates the space she's involved in, has a tremendous local reputation which has taken years to ferment.

The same is true for the likes of Nationwide Building Society, Prudential and Virgin Money, which is why these firms will do well in the artificial intelligence selling market, Robo advising and arti type chatbots. Nationwide dealt with a massive proportion of its chat enquiries over payment-holidays using its automated chat service.

You may not be so lucky to have such a brand behind you. You may not be known at all in your marketplace, so you need to work hard and spend time on building trust and your reputation.

Here's a reminder on how to do that:

- Sprinkle your credibility all over social media and the internet. Make sure your LinkedIn profile is full, blogs are populated with your writings, and your YouTube Channel has some excellent videos about you and your service.

- Have a Zoom background with your certificates and exam rewards.

- Ensure your testimonials are gathered somewhere for people to see. Your website or better still, a third-party site such as vouchedfor, or unbiased.co.uk or www.financiable.co.uk

- Nail the three secrets to trust – common ground, credibility and intent.

- Matching is a great place to start. I have videos on this topic on my YouTube Channel www.paularcher.tv – or just become a little bit like your customer. On a video, that means facial expressions, eye contact matching, voice matching, pace and energy.

- Outlining your intentions is often forgotten. Ensure your customer knows what you're about, why do you do what you do. How your sales process works, how long you'll speak for and so on. Signpost your video calls, so customers know where you're going.

- Learn to be a masterful communicator online.

High trust is paramount but can be broken in an instance, look at Dominic Cummings.

5 Motivators That Influence

I've mentioned before that I help to run a village rugby team and this season the boys all turned 14.

I've helped to coach them since they were under 7s. After a terrible start to the season, with three hammerings on the trot against Stroud, Hereford and Cheltenham, we discovered our form and began to achieve consecutive victories.

What caused the turnaround? We had inadvertently satisfied the 5 top motivators that inspire people.

We obtained 2 new coaches who brought in some new tactics, which made it easier to play. We made the boys wear shirts and club ties after each match and sit down in the clubhouse to eat the sausage and chips together as a team. We continuously applauded their efforts, fed their strengths and made them feel good.

The 5 motivators we'd unconsciously satisfied were:

1. Importance
2. Appreciation
3. Approval
4. Ease
5. Success

So if you coach people, manage teams, manage clients and customers…are you stroking the 5 motivators to influence?

Deliberately now, we try to satisfy these motivators with the boys and we made it to the semi-finals of the North Midlands Plate. Whoever said attitude is more powerful than techniques deserves a pint. And that's exactly what we coaches do in the clubhouse whilst the boys gorge their tucker. Mine's a pint please.

Conciseness Is The Future

"I didn't have time to prepare a long speech" - Churchill.

When presenting at sales meetings or in board rooms, it's good to be concise – time is the key element. Here are some ideas to be more concise.

- 30 seconds answer maximum to all questions at the Q&A.

- Be concise when introducing yourself – keep it to 30 seconds.

- When presenting information, learn to pause and stop waffling; just bite your tongue.

- Stop earlier in sentences than you normally would.

- If they want more information, they'll ask.

- Keep information to one page.

- Slides to a minimum, Google Pecha Kucha if you want to try something quicker and punchier with PowerPoint - http://www.pechakucha.org/

- If they're quiet, it means they got it, so move on to your next topic.

Persuading Customers Through Touch

In NLP we have this concept called anchoring which, like Pavlov's Dogs, allow you to attach a signal to a feeling. Pavlov rang a bell and made his dogs salivate.

But a lot of people know that story.

Natural anchors are sprinkled throughout your life. A special perfume aroma brings back a memory, smells work well and my favourite is gasoline which reminds me of cutting grass when I was 16 for some very rich people who owned a mansion and had au pairs sunbathing in the garden. Now that memory makes me feel good.

Sounds do the same; a tune reminds you of a holiday, an event. The Olympic logo helps people have positive feelings about GB and the country we live in.

I help customers create anchors to relive experiences where they had a particularly good state of mind which they would like again. These are often physical anchors such as a touch of the ear lobe or pressing a knuckle or pushing the oyster on the back of the head. If you don't know where that is, ask a sniper.

Sorry about that pattern interrupt; I caught you, though.

Today I'd like to share with you how you can use anchors with a customer that are so subtle yet impressively powerful.

Let me explain.

Touch is an incredibly powerful signal and touching people creates an electric current that literally zips through people. So here's the drill.

When you meet someone; a customer, a coachee, a stranger and you want to know their name, ask them and at the same time, smile broadly with locked-on eye contact, then lean across and touch them between the elbow and shoulder of their right arm. This touch has now begun to be anchored and there's a connection between the two of you. The anchor you've created has good resonance, their name, you, big smile, eye contact – good feelings.

Now use this touch again when you want to recreate that good experience and positive state. Perhaps when you've presented your solution or idea you could lean across, touch their arm and say, "Can you feel how good this could be for you?"

Or you might want them to make a decision, so lean across and touch their anchored point and say, "Take your time with this important decision, it does feel right though, don't you think?"

The Garden Centre Sales Parallel

Soon after the draconian lockdown restrictions were lifted earlier this year, Shelley and I visited a garden centre to replenish our herbaceous borders. We were expecting the worst experience but were pleasantly surprised.

The GCA – Garden Centre Association – had given extensive guidance on how to handle social distancing and the centre embraced these to the full.

We had a one-way system which took us around the centre "Ikea" style, and we remained behind the people in front like a slow-moving roller coaster. We were outside, so this helped, but even indoors, we felt completely safe. As a result, we spent and spent and spent.

Slowing us down and letting us browse every display helped. Our need was intense because our herbaceous borders had suffered neglect. But it was the process that encouraged sales.

What about you and your process? Does it encourage more sales? If you're in the mortgage profession or financial advice, do you now have shorter online video meetings rather than the old fashioned two-hour-long interview, thankfully a relic of the past?

Shorter meetings bring more variety. So do you signpost each session to deal with a certain aspect? For example, do you have a 20-minute one based around protection and maybe 20 minutes deciding the type of loan. Later on, it might be 20 minutes to discuss the mortgage offer and inheriting the property by your next of kin. More variety means more sales and more closing.

The secret is to have shorter meetings and more of them, with all the people that matter; each session has a distinct objective and close. The garden centre had border plants, followed by grasses, roses, onto the water feature section, fertilisers and soil feed. All encouraged a sale and a close before moving onto the next step.

Adopt the garden centre secret to your meeting structure, and you won't go far wrong. As for our herbaceous border, it's looking beautiful, ready for the next lockdown period.

A Communication Trade Secret

Everyone likes a trade secret, I know I do.

NLP gives us the thinking styles where people have a preference to think in a certain way, to represent information in a unique manner. Some people prefer to think in a kinaesthetic way, with feelings, touch, reactions. Others prefer auditory with sounds, words, language. Some folk prefer a digital thinking style with logic, processes, and non-sensory. But by far the majority of people, particularly Generation Y, like to think in a visual manner, with pictures, images, colour.

Naturally, everyone can have all four in their heads and can communicate quite comfortably in each mode yet the secret is to realise that people have a preference for one or two.

But where's this useful and how can it help us sell and coach better?

You'll want to pick up your customer's style and then adapt your mode of communication to it. If you do, there's two massive payoffs.

Firstly, talking in their language, using their preferred style helps you become a little like them. Commonality is created on a subtle level.

Secondly, and here's a little known trade secret. Folk find it difficult to distinguish between their thoughts, which are in their own language, and words spoken to them in their language. This means you can speak to them in their language and they'll start to think it's their own thoughts.

Spooky eh?

Which is why embedded commands in hypnotic language work really well. Merely make suggestions within your words, and hey presto, they're influenced.

Promise though, you'll use this with the right integrity, won't you?

How To Test Close to Get Commitment Earlier

Test closes are brilliant ways of testing the water with your customers. We all use them probably without even knowing it as it's something you always hear top-performing influencers doing.

Tell me the difference between these four test closes:

- How do you feel so far?

- How does it look to you so far?

- What are you saying to yourself so far?

- What are you hearing so far?

They all attempt to do the same thing, in other words, test the customers' views and thoughts so you can continue with the meeting. Classic test closing. I wonder which one you tend to use with your clients or when coaching.

And I bet one of them really hit the mark with you, or resonated with you more, or was a question you could personally relate to.

You see the four test closes are carefully scripted to appeal to your thinking style. NLP gives us visual, kinaesthetic, auditory and digital thinking styles and everyone has a preference to think predominantly in one fashion although we're quite capable of using all of them. We just prefer one.

If you can gauge your customer's preferred style, then change your language to suit their favourite. Do start with one of the four test closes from above because it's easy to do so, gets you into the habit and you could start tomorrow, couldn't you?

The best way to calibrate your customer's preferred thinking style is to listen to their language or keep an eye on their eye movements. There's a great article on eye movements in our knowledge bank.

The Art of Making Something Simple To Understand

Isn't that exactly what we want to do when talking with customers or when presenting to a group?

Here's how:

1. Clearly describe what they need to hear only; not what you think they need to know about your topic. There's a big difference.

2. Then gives lots of examples. They accelerate understanding, relate to people's worlds and make the unfamiliar…familiar.

3. Finally, make sure you provide lots of visuals, even if it is a flipchart drawing.

Why is it sometimes, you just get things, you understand something? These three steps will let you have the same power.

Staying Alive – How to Make Your Message Stick

Last summer, a grandfather who suffered a heart attack on a bus was saved by a passenger who performed CPR on him whilst singing the Bee Gees "Staying Alive".

For those of you, in the know, you'll recall this was a TV commercial hit starring Vinny Jones, who promoted to conduct CPR to the now-famous tune.

So how is this connected to business presentations and sales? I'll explain.

The TV ad used the ingredients that a true presenter should use when giving a message to an audience. It used:

- Music – the Staying Alive track is upbeat and easy to sing along to.

- Visual – the images of London "Geezer" Gangster Vinny and his accomplices.

- Movement – continuous movement of the scene.

- Comedy – it is very funny.

- My message is to use these ingredients in your presenting.

- Music - don't necessarily use music but provide an aural stimulus.

- Visual – definitely get more visual and I don't mean more PowerPoint slides, I mean props, real images, Prezi.

- Movement – add plenty of kinaesthetic movement to your presenting, not by you, but by your audience or group.

- Comedy – enjoy yourself, have fun, don't take everything too seriously. Go along with the humour of the group, tell amusing stories.

And if you want to enjoy the clip, go to YouTube and search for Vinny Jones, British Heart Foundation. It's a hoot and saved Terry Holly's life. Well done BHF and Vinny.

Hot Buttons

When it comes down to it, people do things for five reasons – security, comfort, peace, power and convenience. I'm into comfort and convenience and these drive my behaviour and my motivation.

So if you're looking to influence someone towards your idea, finding these "hot buttons" is vital as part of the pacing process. But how do you do this? By asking questions, so let me explain.

There's two questions to ask.

Firstly "What's important to you about (insert issue)?"

Probe further by asking "Why is that important to you?"

You might have to ask a few times but you will arrive at a hot button or value.

For example, I want to influence a member of my team to think about their career direction and maybe take up a promotion that's coming up, so I would start by asking:

"What's important to you about your career?"

"What else?"

"Why is that important?"

And these will reveal the driver behind the issue. You won't get them saying power or those words – it'll be their own description and that's fine.

Now you can use these values when you pitch your idea and you can appeal to the emotional side because that's how people make decisions and that's how you influence. Afterwards they can justify them logically.

By the way, security is green, comfort is blue and yellow, peace is also yellow and blue, power is red. Convenience could be all of them.

Stories and Metaphors

I love a story don't you? I think we all do as it floods back memories of childhood listening to engaging stories or friends at a party telling us a humorous interlude in their life.

I love the detail of a good yarn, one that captures my attention. A thrilling film, which is a story brought to life, a funny report in the newspaper, a snippet from a friend in the pub.

Stories are part of life and very hypnotic indeed. So much so because a good story bypasses the conscious mind, the part which applies beliefs or analysis, and lets us relax and enjoy the lesson.

And if we see a parallel to our current lives, we spot it immediately, at least our subconscious does and acts accordingly.

You see that's how influencers should use stories. Carefully craft your story, memory or metaphor to solve the problem of a customer. Preserve the structure of the problem but change the story.

Remember to itemise the customer's pain or problem that you've established through questions and conversation. Then rather than tell your customer what's what, tell them through a carefully crafted story, maintaining the problem but being adventurous with the description.

For example, you talk about protecting the customer during an insurance sale and you've encouraged them to see how it might be if one of them had a terrible accident and couldn't work, so you tell a story.

"I was on duty so to speak, refereeing a junior rugby match with my Under 12s one wet and cold Sunday morning. The northerly wind was swirling in over the playing fields, mums and dads with flasks of hot coffee huddled in their overcoats and onto the field trudged our team.

At age 12 they represent all sorts of sizes and shapes. Some lads develop early as testosterone kicks in, some fail to grow at all and that one little lad was Matt. A tiny slender frame of a boy but refreshingly happy and eager to play every Sunday. Always chatty and excited and often the first to the breakdown.

After just 2 minutes the opposition kicked the ball into our half and Matt, as always was the first to the ball. Matt only knew one direction…that was forward and within seconds was surrounded by about 6 of their players and soon after was joined by about 6 of ours to form a maul.

Pushing and shoving, yanking and pulling, the maul was going nowhere but just before I blew the whistle, the maul collapsed. When mauls collapse, pounds of human flesh and bones pile on top of each other. Poor Matt was on the bottom of the pile and couldn't move. After a short while and a dose of the wet sponge, he was led to the sidelines where he sat bewildered and bruised. He lived to tell the story with no broken bones, but he couldn't get to school the next day or a few days after that.

The next day his Dad emailed me to explain that Matt didn't want to play rugby anymore as the bashing and bruising that he got every Sunday was just too much and he was regularly missing school. I hadn't been aware of this until then and I wholeheartedly agreed with his dad's wishes.

But what about mild bashes and bruises, how would they affect your ability to go to work, or maybe an illness or a more serious accident?"

Keep the fabric of the problem intact, change the story, embellish it, bring it to life and your customer will see the parallels of the story and know the lesson.

To bring your story to life, it has to be true – one that you've personally experienced. Remember the details, the fine points, they make all the difference. Follow this structure:

1. Set the scene (remember my cold wet Sunday morning refereeing rugby)

2. Introduce the character (can you see Matt in your mind's eye?)

3. Go on a journey (Matt caught the ball and headed straight into the group of players)

4.   Have an obstacle to overcome (getting through the maul safely and with the ball)

5.   The phrase that pays (how would bashes and bruises affect your ability to earn a living with bills to pay?)

Once you begin to think stories, you can craft stories to fit most parts of the sales process. Overcoming objections works well. Use feel, felt, found…

"I see how you feel about that Brian, in fact a customer of mine last week felt the same way as you…let me tell you their story…."

A story to show what you do and how you work differently to the competition, can be a great ice breaker. Think of metaphors i.e. our after-sales service is just like an Olympic Gold Medal Ice Skating routine.

Remember stories go straight to the heart of the matter, they by-pass the usual analytical side and people just love them, don't you?

Anchoring your Customer

Here's a neat little idea to boost your confidence and energy levels, and let's face it, we all need to do this sometimes.

We've all come across the term "anchoring" where we use a reminder or a trigger to recall something from the past. NLP or Neuro-Linguistic Programming brings this to us and it helps us to relive past moments in our lives so we can collect the resource that we had in abundance at the time.

I have several anchors which I use to inject myself with a resource. For example, before a big presentation I recall a specific moment where I collect huge amounts of enthusiasm. If I want to relax I have an anchor that does just that. They're pretty much like speed dials on your phone; they just take you back to when you had that resource in abundance and trick the brain to feel the same way again. The more you fire up the anchor the more reactive it is.

Here's an idea when you want to help your customer to buy from you.

Take them back to a time when they bought something really successfully, get them to relive the moment, the emotions, the sights.

Ask them to recall it in their minds' eye, describe it, why they made the purchase.

When they're really in the zone, anchor it with a sound, a physical gesture or a subtle touch on their elbow. As you approach the time for them to buy your product, bring back the sound or the gesture or do the touch.

I've used this whilst coaching. I've asked my coachee to think back to a time when they were self-sufficient, could handle anything themselves, were tremendously resourceful and action-oriented. I usually anchor this with a change in my position – I use the catapult position where I lean back and put my hands behind my head and at the same time say the phrase "good for you". Later in our coaching session I might want them to take some action or be resourceful. I redo the catapult gesture, smile, say "good for you" and wait.

It often works and they become resourceful and full of action plans, which is the goal of the coaching.

So try anchoring your customer or coachee next time and see if it makes a difference. And you can thank Neuro-Linguistic Programming for that.

Covert Anchoring

My audiences know that I move around the stage for a purpose, not randomly. I'll tell you more about this shortly because it's a clever influencing technique to move an audience to agree with your idea or proposal.

It's all to do with spatial anchoring – now that's another NLP term they took from the top drawer of dictionaries. Anchoring is merely a way to recall a state of mind from some kind of memory jog.

We've been doing this for centuries. The smell of grass floods back pleasant memories of working in people's gardens when I was a young teenager earning my first paycheque. The smell makes me feel good. Photos from past holidays bring back happy memories.

We know this and I bet all of you have similar anchors.

But where's this going to be useful when influencing people? Let me explain.

Firstly we have to do it subtly or in a covert manner. After all, we don't want our customer to know what we're up to, do we?

Now think what kind of state of mind we want our customer to get into when we influence them. You might pick decisiveness. That would be jolly useful since they're more than likely to be in a position to make a quick decision to our advantage.

So pace them carefully, match their physiology and other aspects you choose. Once you have the rapport, get them into the state you want. For decisiveness you might want to ask them to go back to a time when they made a really good decision. Explore it with them, probe more, listen intently and when you think they're immersed in the state of mind, create the anchor or memory jogger.

You might choose something visual or auditory. A facial expression on your part, a gesture maybe or a distinctive tone in your voice. Or both. I often use a touch at this point, subtly touching their shoulder. Or sometimes I'll raise my right hand and twist it slowly in front of them.

For me, when I'm on the training stage I create a timeline along the stage, from my right to my left. Seen by the audience I have a timeline which starts on their left and continues along the stage to their right. Most people have times or diaries which go from left to right. I create this by running through the agenda with them at the beginning, starting on their left and moving slowly across the stage until I hit their right. I then move to the position when I'm talking about something that happened in the past. You guessed it, I'm standing on their left hand side of the stage, where the time came from.

Subtly I've anchored the stage for them. The left hand side is the past and their right hand side is the future.

Once you've created this anchor, you fire it off when you want them to have the state of mind.

When I'm presenting my proposal I'll subtly touch them on their shoulder or raise my right hand and slowly twist it. And when I'm presenting my proposal and mentioning the competition, I'll casually walk over to the "past" - their left hand side of the stage. And the past is well, passed.

And when I mention my idea, yep…I walk over to their right – their future anchored state.

Provocative Objection Handling

Handling customer reservations does rather smack of 1990s influencing techniques. I prefer to deal with the problems and issues earlier on rather than at the end. This technique works whether you're influencing a product or an idea. You probably know what the issues are going to be, so raise them early and deal with them then.

But occasionally, a lingering problem might rear its head once you've asked for the order or proposed your idea to the customer.

If so, try provocative objection handling, it might just work.

Let me explain.

They throw up a problem or barrier. Instead of dealing with it, don't. Just say something like: "Do you know perhaps you're just not right for this idea, just not ready. It's OK, this idea is not for everyone and maybe it's not for you."

Now wait for a reaction. They'll respond quickly and probably tell you that everything else is fine about the idea. Now they're on the back foot and will defend the fact that they are right for the idea.

It does work.

And if it doesn't… then maybe they weren't right for the idea or the product and you can move onto the next person. Sometimes we have nothing to lose.

How To Handle Meetings In Busy Crowded Areas

Do you ever have to meet clients or colleagues in crowded areas to have a meeting. Starbucks, busy hotel lobbies, reception areas, service stations. Unfortunately it's the sign of the times and we don't always have the privacy of a room. Read on and I'll share some ideas on how you can get the best out of these meetings.

I could just see the Prudential logo on her notepad so I guessed she was a financial adviser meeting with a prospective client in a hotel reception in deepest darkest Suffolk.

Quite normal you might say but little did she know that I was about to start a multi room conference at the same hotel with about 60 delegates milling between half a dozen rooms on two floors with break outs planned every 15 minutes. The reception area was going to become a bit like Piccadilly Circus on steroids.

I did feel sorry for her…and her client…and I was tempted to pop over and give her some tips to handle the situation she found herself in.

Backs to the Wall

In heavy interruption areas such as coffee shops, hotel lobbies, reception areas, try and put yourself with your back to a wall or blank area so your client doesn't get distracted whilst watching you. You can then use all sorts of gestures and non verbal language to get your points across. You might get distracted but you can handle that can't you?

Spatial Anchoring

Use your body language and gestures to keep more attention than just your voice. Use special anchoring (yes you can get jabs for that at the chemist) to differentiate information. For example when you talk about your competition, move your body one way and for information about you and your service, move your body into a different position. Your client will anchor the information to the body position.

Alternatively use your left and right hands to mean things. "On one hand we could look at this option and on the other hand we could go this way". Now emphasise or gesture the hand you would rather they take. This is quite hypnotic by the way.

The Cooperative Angle

Always sit at 90 degrees to your client as this is known as the cooperative position but remember what's behind you.

Eye Level

Remember your eyes must be level with your client's. This is usually very easy when you're both sitting down but if you're standing up and you're much taller than your client, you could come across as looking down at them. Not good.

Voice Emphasis

Emphasise your voice more to keep their attention. Change your tone…speed up to add excitement to a point and sloooow down to emphasise a decision. Finally, when asking for some commitment or closing, attempt to slow your voice pace and lower your tone. This change in voice is very good at building belief and credibility to your proposition. Try it, it works.

What to do with Hands

Hands? What do we do with them? When sitting down with clients, try to keep your hands below your face and above the table. This is the triangle zone. Keep them in this zone and use gestures but small ones. Hand to face does you no favours at all so keep them away from this area unless you want to do a classic thinking person's pose. Standing to present, keep your hands in the zone between your belly button and chin – never below or above these places. Use them to gesture and describe, don't grasp them like there's no tomorrow.

And with your back to the wall, using your body language to its maximum effect and your voice to gain their attention, so your client can really focus just on you, you're open to a little bit of hypnotic language. But that's for another day.

And my financial adviser guest? No, I didn't pop over to her, that wouldn't be right or well received. Bless her though, she just carried on, but you could plainly see the client was clearly distracted much of the time. Shame that…a couple of these tips might have made all the difference.

Language to Influence

Tainted words

Tainted…contaminated…stained…infected.

These are some words that you really want to stop using in your sales and coaching language but they just seem to pop up everywhere. This chapter will give you an edge in influencing that very few others have.

Signature

Please sign here. Sign your life away you mean. Just stop and think of the impact this has on people. It can terrify some, turn others into objection maniacs or just stop others in their tracks to really question what they're doing.

Think of alternative ways of asking people to sign things. Use autograph, "Can you authorise this form for me please", "Can you kindly OK this for me please".

If you indicate to the customer where they should be signing, keep well away from putting an X marks the spot and use a tick instead. What does the note X mean to people?

Yep it means wrong, zip, zero, bad, you can do better, incorrect.

Obvious when you think about it.

Problems

Use this word at your peril. I often talk about revealing customer problems before introducing a solution and this is a tried and tested consultative selling technique. Just don't use the word "problem". Instead use challenge or issue.

Price

Definitely a no-no. Cheap, even worse and you'll be inviting discounts. Instead re-phrase to cost, investment or fee. They just sound better.

Hesitate

We use the phrase "don't hesitate to contact me". What are people going to do? Yes they're going to hesitate before calling you.

Don't

This morning my 12 year old son Euan was eating his chocolate crispy thingies at breakfast when he suddenly announced to his mum, "Mum, don't think I'm being rude, but do you mind if Dad takes us to school this morning?"

Now how do you feel my wife felt? She felt hurt. Not because she didn't want to take him to school because she's always got a thousand things to do. Not because of being refused. The reason she felt hurt is because she was asked to think that Euan was going to be rude and before she even heard him, she'd convinced herself that he was going to be rude.

And when he wasn't it didn't matter. She'd convinced herself that whatever he was going to say, he was going to be rude.

Strange that. But logical.

You see if I ask you not to do something, the way we process this in our heads is to think of the thing we're not going to do first, then we think of not doing it, as instructed. The net result, we think of doing it.

Don't think now of a giant flying carrot.

And what do you think of? A giant flying carrot!

Keep an eye on your conversation over the next day or so and listen out for the "don'ts" and "nots". Most of us, me included, sprinkle our language with them.

In sales this can be disastrous.

"Don't worry about the price yet".

"It doesn't matter that we can't deliver on that day because we can…".

"With our product, you won't ever need to worry about competitors' products".

There's a few for you to be getting on with in our drive to rid the world of tainted words.

Embedded Suggestions

Remember earlier I explained that hypnotic influencing is simply the art of occupying the front brain and then slipping in commands into the back door i.e. the subconscious. Well this is exactly where embedded commands come into their own.

Like the stage hypnotist who'll put you into a trance and then tell you to jump around like a donkey or blow a raspberry at the audience…in influencing we make more subtle commands.

These are words or short phrases that we slip in with our normal conversation that are ignored but subliminally processed by our customers to have an effect.

Here's some examples:

"I, like many other people, enjoy driving."

"Buy now, Mr Smith, you're wondering what benefits this product gives you…"

"You, like me, enjoy getting value for your money."

"I'm hoping you'll want to place an order right now, but before you do…"

"*Buy* the way; let's have a quick summary of the benefits of this plan."

So there are 5 examples for you of embedded suggestions. You'll notice, like many other people reading this article, that I miss-spelt buy. It should be by. But the reason I did this was to show you that some words have more than one meaning and the brain has to process all the various meanings before it arrives at the right one. So the customer is thinking about buying without knowing it.

Also I really want the customer to like me, so I embedded the phrase in and at the same time drove home the fact that I like lots of people. The other phrases are just suggestions that I openly stated.

These all slip under the radar or into the subconscious and start working for you.

Throw Rocks…

In his latest book "Buying Trances", Dr Joe Vitale talks about the 5 Keys ultimate persuasion techniques. These are really powerful and have been used by cult leaders, political dictators and many ruthless individuals to ensure the following of thousands of people.

People will do anything for you if you:

1. Allay their fears
2. Help them throw rocks at their enemies
3. Confirm their suspicions
4. Encourage their dreams
5. Justify their failures

But hold on, don't we all have common enemies that both we and our customers have a moan about – the weather, the taxman, the FCA?

And don't we help customers to achieve their goals and growth objectives and I guess we encourage their dreams? And if they're wary of using our service or product, do we not overcome their concerns to help them become more comfortable?

Perhaps we're cut out to be a cult leader after all.

A Logical Way to Move Your Client Forward

Do you think it makes sense to…

Here's a little bit of gold dust for you when it comes to closing or moving your customer to the next stage of your sales process. Appeal to their sense of logic.

"Do you think it makes sense to…"

"Do you think it's a logical step to…"

For example, you want your customer to agree on a discovery meeting with you for 15 minutes after an introductory phone call. "Do you think it makes sense now to schedule a 15-minute discovery zoom or phone call where we can talk about your situation in more detail?"

It is much better than, "Shall we fix up a call?"

Do you think it makes sense? Logical, compelling and somewhat hypnotic.

Scientific Influencing

Cialdini's 6 Principles

Made famous by Robert Cialdini.

The purpose of this article is not to repeat what Robert wrote about, but to show you my take on the topic and how you can use these principles in your everyday influencing. I'll also use my prospecting engine as an example. This is how I generate new business for my firm and the same engine can be used by you if you sell knowledge and expertise.

Onto the first principle

Reciprocity

This is the most powerful so it comes first. Quite simply if you provide something of value to someone that they weren't expecting and didn't ask for…then they will have an uncontrollable urge to return the favour sometime. And that favour might be to agree to your idea or proposal.

In my prospecting engine, when a customer starts flowing through my sales funnel, I'll post them a signed copy of my book. This has value. To prove it, the physical cost of postage and the book comes to around £20. Now I don't know what value a signature has, but it sure does wrap it up perfectly.

The cost to me is very little but the reciprocity is powerful.

Liking

My favourite which works with my personality. It's not essential to like someone to do business or work with in a business setting…but it does help. When people are like each other, they like each other. We've known this for years.

My sales funnel includes a prospective client meeting when I meet them face to face, I will always spend my own dollar to go and see new clients, so long as I've qualified them. When we're face to face, I focus on the liking. I match and mirror ferociously to build rapport, matching physiology and energy levels. This isn't mimicking, its cementing our connection, after all, if we both like each other, it's so much easier to do business. I give genuine compliments and use humour. These are all ingredients of liking. I do a little touch if appropriate too.

Social Proof

Malcom Gladwell has quoted that in life, about 95% of people are followers and 5% are leaders. Followers follow the lead of others. If people like me also like the product or idea, then I'll like it too.

The proliferation of reviews dominate our internet searching.

In my prospecting engine I use social proof throughout. In my incubator, I use social media particularly LinkedIn to show what others think of my work. I have 1,200 people I'm linked in to, all within my sector and expertise area.

I have client case studies which clearly show what value other companies have received. My website is littered with customer testimonials from products I sell. And above all, about 60% of all my new business is from referrals from clients and my network, which clearly shows social proof.

Authority

Gladwell's quote works well here too. People respect authority and follow it. There are 4 aspects to creating authority that people will follow:

- Titles
- Clothing
- Trappings or bling
- Expertise

Now you may have all four of these and if so, you've created authority and many will follow you.

In my prospecting engine I use expertise. Yes I'll wear a suit, my favourite watch and drive a decent car to the client's car park. That can set a frame that you're expensive, so you need to tread carefully here. To be honest, these trappings don't sit well with me but expertise does.

Expertise starts in my incubator as I drench my database in my expertise. I write mercilessly creating weekly additions to my four blogs. I have long form articles on LinkedIn, Ezinearticles.com. I've published four books with the fifth one due next year. I've niched my expertise as far as I can and have particular expertise in the area of professional services i.e. influencing knowledge. And I have over 35 years' experience of this sector.

I'm not blowing my trumpet – typical English reserve – but I am an expert and I use this to evolve this influencing technique.

Scarcity

For scarcity to work, you've got to be busy or at least, get busy in your head. Then you can create scarcity for your ideas or time. People are drawn to things that are scarce. When not everyone can have it, people want it badly. Limited offers, sale on for just 3 days, whilst stocks last.

For me, I create scarcity by not being available. And this is genuinely true. I am busy and I can't be everywhere all the time. I will carefully qualify people that enter my sales funnel. If they are not in my sector, don't have budget or capability to make decisions about training and development, then they can't enter the funnel. And I'll say this upfront, people respect it, they see I'm valuable and scarce. I have a select group of clients and don't work with everyone, which is why referrals are my main source of new business because it ticks scarcity, social proof, expertise, reciprocity and liking.

Oh, and my written proposals expire after 7 days.

Contrast

Finally the principle of contrast. Place your idea next to something else and the contrast created points towards your idea. In my prospecting engine I use contrast when giving the investment. I will provide three solutions – very high value, very high cost, medium and low. Clients often choose the middle one because the high one creates the contrast.

CRASSL

- Contrast

- Reciprocity

- Authority

- Scarcity

- Social Proof

- Liking

And if you want to see all 6 in action, a great film is Boiler Room and the scene when Seth Davis sells some stocks over the phone from a cold call. It's here on YouTube: https://www.youtube.com/watch?v=eY4UVrXzyhE

Whisper To Be Believed

Do you know, if you whisper something to someone, the chances are they'll believe you more. It's psychology and it works too.

I'm not saying we need to start lying, heavens forbid. But I am saying to influence someone with your idea or notion, try whispering the idea and you'll be more persuasive.

It makes sense really. When we whisper people lean forward to be able to hear you. It appears that whatever it is you're going to say, is not for public broadcasting so it's important as well as true.

You could use this technique:

- When you're observing and coaching on a field visit, try giving your feedback in a whisper

- In presentations, occasionally lower your voice for important messages and if you're miked up, whisper for extra influence.

- With customers, lower your voice when you're coming to present your solution and if you're close to them and in a quiet place, whisper for extra influence.

Shhhh…don't tell anyone else.

Would You Like To Try One Sir?

Do you know they spring up almost everywhere where people have time to kill. What am I talking about? The kind of shops at airports and train stations where you buy stuff you don't really need because you have an hour or so to kill.

Last month at Paddington Station in London, I had an hour to waste and was wandering around with nothing to do until I saw a shop that caught my eye. A tiny little place that seemed to sell every nut possible in a Pick 'n Mix style. Now I'm partial to a nut I have to say, so I popped my head in to have a look, not wanting to commit myself, since I had started a diet that week.

The array of nuts looked appetising but I was about to turn away to find something healthier and less calorific to eat, like some celery, when the shop assistant caught my eye.

She smiled, said "how are you today" and "care to try some honey covered pecan nuts for free?" Of course I did and boy were they tasty.

I felt obliged to walk into the shop, browse and bought a whole bag of mixed nuts, found a little corner of the station to nest into and wolfed the lot.

Now in sales, this little lady used one of the greatest influencing techniques ever known to mankind. The principle of reciprocity or using the power of reciprocation to build a sale. By giving me a smile and some free nuts, this powered up the in-built "click whir" human reaction of reciprocating or giving something back in return. And it worked. I spent £4 on a small bag of nuts.

My wife has a huge network of other mums and they are always reciprocating with each other to help each other out, constantly returning favours.

In sales, we should consider how we can give something to our customers to build this yearning to reciprocate. Samples, corporate days out, information, newsletters, competitor analysis, training staff, sales aids, lunch….the list goes on. Think of something you can give to your customer that is valuable to them. Give it freely with no obligation and I guarantee you'll start their internal clock to reciprocate to you sometime.

I have to say though, if you ever pass a little nut shop at Paddington Station, you simply have to try the honey covered pecans – they are to die for.

Building Demand with Scarcity

What does Glastonbury Festival 2008 have to do with a very smart influencing tactic? Read on and I'll explain.

It was snowing heavily outside as I fell out of bed, thump. I reached for my laptop and sat up trying to stir myself from a gorgeous sleep.

It was Glastonbury Festival time. In 10 minutes I was going to log onto the special site to see if I could be one of the chosen few to get Glasto tickets for 2008. The lottery started at 9am and previous years had seen tickets sell out in 30 minutes flat and much disappointment for me.

You see Glastonbury festival is probably one the most well known brands alive and each year their festival is flocked to by thousands of fans. They operate one of the most effective influencing techniques going – that of scarcity. You can use this when you're influencing.

Make something scarce and people will want it. It's human nature to want something you can't have and Glastonbury tickets are like gold dust.

They do it so well. I mean create scarcity. Firstly they have a great product, secondly you have to register one month beforehand with your photograph and thirdly the tickets go on sale online at a certain time on a certain date. The organisers make it known that each year 10 or 12 times the number of successful people apply, thousands are disappointed, like me for the last three years.

Which creates a huge demand for the product.

Clever, huh?

So think about your service and products. Naturally you are good at what you do and your products are first class but are they scarce? Is your time scarce? Could you:

- Put deadlines on special deals
- Put maximum numbers that can be bought

- "Whilst stocks last"

- "Sale ends Friday"

- Make appointments at 10.25 rather than 10 o'clock to appear scarce

- Say no to the customer's first choice of appointment because you are busy with other clients

- Demonstrate your expertise via client testimonials

- Say things like "I can only fit in 3 client meetings each day"

Don't be arrogant about things but make your product and service scarce and popular and clients will want it more.

And what happened on that snowy Sunday morning? Frustration, annoyance; I couldn't log on and a desire to want a ticket raged inside me.

Suddenly I was in. The registration page appeared which I swiftly filled in, and hey presto, I was successful and I'm going to Glastonbury.

But the ironic thing? I heard this morning that there are tickets still available, and on sale again on a date next week. They weren't that scarce after all! But I was sucked into the hype.

Scarcity Is a Great Tip Unless You're Desperate.

We all know that the use of scarcity can increase the desire for our product or service. Letting prospective customers know there's only a limited time available or little left only exacerbates demand. Amazon use it "only 3 left in stock", hotel sites use it "10 people have been looking at this hotel in the last hour"

But what happens to scarcity when you're desperate. Despairing for the next sale and scarcity drops out the window. This can give the wrong message, and I thought so, until I read the following board outside a bistro hotel in Stow on the Wold last weekend.

That's how you do it. Turn it into a positive. Never admit a weakness, desperation for business. Customers can sniff this a mile away.

15 Influencing Techniques Crammed in One Presentation

Morrisons Supermarket – UK – June 2015

My curiosity was piqued with a warm, exciting voice-over in the store announcement. He seemed upbeat and different to the usual droning voices announcing cut price bread and prawns on special.

He offered us a no catch, free gift if we went to row 9 to his presentation podium. Attraction.

He presented the knives in the middle of the narrow isle to create a crowd, which drew people's curiosity.

He gathered us round his podium and began to demonstrate how good his knives were with some pretty clever displays. Social proof and crowds.

He didn't sell at all, just demonstrated at first.

His company was a very important company from America, who were importing the product for the first time and had been operating for many years. Authority.

Reciprocity. He gave out free small gifts to the audience if they answered a question or raised their hands the fastest.

He continually promised us the free knife at the end of the presentation. Temptation.

He got the audience involved to create tension and interest.

He had some fun and some witty one-liners to keep our attention. Entertainment.

He overcame objections by building them into his pitch. For example, why would you want more than one knife if they have a lifetime guarantee?

He showed us a lifetime guarantee on the product he was demonstrating, the guarantee was a laminated certificate that looked very authentic. Removing risk.

Scarcity. He teased us with the product by saying that it was from America, they were going to advertise next month so we were the first to be offered the opportunity to buy them, before the masses were invited.

He packaged the knives into a collection which we could buy, rather than individual knives.

Scarcity. He said he was only allowed to sell 7 of the knife collections right now as the company wouldn't allow any more.

Contrast. He gave us the normal prices first before revealing today's special offer price. The normal price was in the two hundred pounds mark, today only price was £40.

He made it easy for us to buy the product by allowing us to simply put it in our shopping trolley.

And he sold 7 knife sets, and I bought one too.

Most Of My Clients…

75% of people who stay in this room, use the same towels to save detergent and energy.

We've all seen these signs in hotel bathrooms using the science of influencing and they do work, only this week I used the same towel four times.

Do you use the same concept in your business?

- 75% of my clients are able to make a referral of one of their contacts to me.

- 75% of people who buy this product are also interested in this one.

- 75% of my mortgage clients take life cover to protect themselves.

- 75% of people upgrade to the silver level.

I just hope the hotel don't use the same towel as the person who stayed in the room before me.

Making Your Product Appear Scarce

What's your favourite Sunday roast joint? Beef, chicken, lamb? We asked our three children at the beginning of the year which they preferred and unanimously they said pork. The salesman in me made me ask a few questions as to why and immediately they all replied, "We love the crackling, the meat's just OK."

And when I asked them which meat they preferred, they admitted they weren't really keen on pork as a meat, they actually preferred chicken but they'd choose pork every time as they adored the crackling.

The only problem is that there isn't much of it, I wish there were more. Crackling that is. It is a scarce resource.

So how do you combine chicken with crackling to create the perfect Sunday roast? Well you can and we did. We bought some crackling on its own as a roll from Morrisons – cost 88p – and cooked it alongside the chicken in the oven for a very special Sunday lunch. The children called it Crackin.

Apparently the court of Henry VIII used to do it all the time – that is, mix meats together in a joint. Weird.

The dinner was going to be a huge success – chicken with pork crackling. Yum yum.

Following enormous portions of chicken and crackling, we tucked in. The meal was eerily quiet, no one said a word just lots of crunching. The children didn't finish off their plates and the crackling bowl was hardly touched.

I couldn't understand it until Euan said "Dad it was nice but there was too much there and I didn't fancy it, sorry Dad."

And this made me think of one of the most famous persuasion tactics known to mankind – that of scarcity. When something is scarce we want it – but when something becomes plentiful we lose interest.

The makers of fruit pastilles did this years ago. The most favourite of all the coloured pastilles was the black one – they researched thoroughly and found out that the majority of people loved the black pastille more than all the other colours and people would even discard the others until they reached the coveted black one.

Rowntrees came up with a packet of black only pastilles and expected a hit. Just like my crackling idea, it flopped – suddenly they were plentiful and demand fell and soon after they withdrew them from the shops.

Think about what you do. Do you sell a product or service, do you coach people on a 1 to 1 basis? Think how you can make this scarce? Picking up on the coaching side, could you not have so many dates available for coaching? Could you limit the time you coach? Might you not be able to coach someone this week because your diary is full?

If you negotiate, don't be too keen to say yes immediately, hold back a little, and don't provide everything they want. Limit numbers, quantity, explain you're waiting for delivery because the product is so very popular.

Remember scarcity makes anything appear more valuable and drives up demand. Position your product, service or idea that you're influencing, so it appears precious by making it appear scarce.

And the crackling, whatever happened to that? It was a damp squib. In fact the children have gone off crackling altogether which is not such a bad thing really. Just looking at the stuff makes your arteries harden.

Sunshine and Scarcity

I'm writing this piece in the garden in August. The sun is beating down on me, its 30 degrees and sweltering. I'm enjoying the sun even more because I know by tomorrow it'll be gone. Replaced by the pervasive cloud and rain. Seasonal weather for the UK.

Why do people rock up on their Mediterranean holidays and get sunburnt in the first few days? Because they know the sun is going to go away when they get home, they gorge on it.

Sunshine is lovelier when you know it's not going to last. If you live in Dubai or Southern Spain, it's not adored so much because you get it virtually every day without fail.

This is important is selling.

Something that's scarce is more desirable. So the objective is to make whatever it is you're selling more attractive by making it appear scarce.

If you're in the professional advising game, this means:

- Limiting the number of clients you can take on and letting your prospective client know that.

- Making your time challenging to obtain.

- Rationing your time to individual clients. 30 minutes maximum appointment.

- Be prepared to walk away and become unavailable. If your new enquiry volunteers that they're shopping around, let them do so and remove yourself from their shopping list. Explain that you're not right for everyone and probably not a fit for them. They'll come back wanting more.

These are just some ideas; I'm sure you have many more.

I just wish I had more sunshine on offer today; some black clouds are coming over the horizon. It looks like rain will stop play.

Provocative Objection Handling

Handling customer reservations does rather smack of 1990s selling techniques. I prefer to deal with the problems and issues earlier than at the end. This technique works whether you're selling a product or an idea. You probably know the problems, so raise them early and deal with them then.

But occasionally, a lingering problem might rear its head once you've asked for the order or proposed your idea to the customer.

If so, try provocative objection handling; it might just work.

Let me explain.

They throw up a problem or barrier. Instead of dealing with it, don't. Just say something like: "Do you know, perhaps you're just not right for this idea, just not ready. It's OK, this idea is not for everyone, and maybe it's not for you."

Now, wait for a reaction. They'll respond quickly and probably tell you that everything else is fine about the idea. Now they're on the back foot and defend that they are suitable for the concept.

It does work. It uses the Cialdini influencing principle of scarcity.

And if it doesn't… then maybe they weren't appropriate for the idea or the product, and you can move on to the next person. Sometimes we have nothing to lose.

Influencing Is Full of Contrast

One of the greatest treasures of family life is the traditional Sunday roast we orchestrate every Sunday. It's a chance to sit down, catch up with the week, share your highs and lows and be injected with all the vitamins you need to sustain life for the next week.

And you can imagine our horror, when my wife announced at the end of November that we weren't going to have roasts anymore until Christmas Day.

We stared aghast; we couldn't believe what we were hearing, until she announced that we would enjoy our Christmas dinner even more than ever before.

Now my wife has never had training is persuasion or influencing but she had used one of the most powerful influencing strategies ever created – contrast.

Where do you use contrast to influence your customers? Where can you encourage action by adopting a contrast strategy?

Many years ago when I worked in real estate agency, we would use a stooge property to show customers first before revealing the one we wanted to sell. This stooge property was usually in need of repair and redecoration, so when they arrived at the chosen home, it just appeared better in contrast. Bad, I know but at least you know in case an agent uses the trick with you.

Life is full of contrast, how do you use it with your customers?

And yes, the Christmas dinner that year at the Archers was to die for and everyone admitted it just tasted so more yummy this year than previous years. My wife gave us a wry smile.

The Most Powerful Persuasion Technique Known

At the tender age of 12, I became a paperboy. At the crack of dawn, I cycled around my estate delivering newspapers to sleeping customers. Throughout the winter it was dark, cold and early.

It wasn't always dark. In the summer it was gloriously bright and sunny even at 5am in the morning, but as the year progressed it became darker in the mornings. October was the turning point for me; I awoke in the pitch blackness of night. I had some brief respite when the clocks went backwards at the end of October; this gave me daylight again for a few weeks.

This was a revelation and a real pick me up. However by mid-November, the darkness crept up once again and greeted me in the morning.

I didn't know at the time but I'd discovered the most powerful persuasion technique known. Let me explain.

You see I didn't see morning daylight again until mid-March and it made me want it even more.

I had a problem and then I got what I wanted, then it was taken away and this drove me to want it even more.

This is the most powerful persuasion technique ever known. Do you use it in your influencing and coaching?

We used to call it the puppy dog technique. Give the child the puppy for the weekend and ask for it back on Monday morning. Guaranteed the child would want it even more after it was taken away.

If you coach your people, give them superb coaching, then take it away when they start to like it. That way they'll be clamouring for more.

When you're about to spend good money on a new car, the canny sales companies lend you the same car over the entire weekend. We had this a little while ago and spent the whole weekend driving around enjoying the new wheels. By the Monday, when it was collected by the dealer, we desperately wanted to buy it.

If you sell card payment chip and pin machines to retailers, do you paint such a picture that they can feel and breathe the image of extra customer takings and the smiles on their new customers' faces as they swiftly pay by card instead of reaching for their cash?

If you sell travel insurance, can your customer imagine what it's like on the airplane travelling to their holiday destination with that warm feeling that if anything happened they'd be treated with dignity by the hospital at their destination at no charge?

The perfect mortgage and protection package. Paint the picture of an impeccable home and security of ownership…

And then take the idea away and await the customer's reaction. They'll want it more.

Much to my relief, Spring did arrive for me as a paperboy but the following year I was promoted to writing addresses on the papers in the shop. Light, warm and dry. I was paid more too, and no more cycling around the estate on those gloomy mornings.

Hypnotic Influencing – Under the Radar

What Is Hypnotic Selling?

Picture it: Springtime in London, amongst 300 people in a giant conference hall just off Tottenham Court Road. I'd just put this guy under. In a deep hypnotic trance, he was and I played my part as the hypnotist.

Upon the stage was Paul McKenna, world-famous stage hypnotist, and he was putting the finishing touches to our hypnosis training as part of my NLP Master Practitioner Programme.

As I brought my colleague back out of his deep trance, I thought to myself, "I don't want to be a hypnotist... I'm a sales trainer... I don't want to carry around a dangling watch and hypnotise people."

But I realised it was all part of the Master Practitioner course, so I continued.

When you think of hypnotism, you think of stage guys like Derren Brown and Paul McKenna or the spoof on Little Britain - Kenny Craig – who was modelled on Paul McKenna.

You don't immediately think of professional selling strategies.

But that's where I was wrong back in 2000. I couldn't see how hypnotism could be used in sales, but now I do and I want to share with you how we can marry the two and give you a substantial edge in your selling ability.

Get Off Your Ego

This week I was teaching some influencers to build rapport and we stumbled across the topic of matching and mirroring. My group pushed back on me and explained that they'd been taught all of that before and found it quite patronising.

They felt it was too basic and that copying someone's body language and imitating their voice was condescending to their customers.

They have a point, they made it very well, and I could see where they were coming from. And within 5 minutes they had a realisation, let me explain what happened to them, you might find it useful yourself.

I've always been fascinated by hypnosis and adore watching TV hypnotists like Paul McKenna, Derren Brown and Kenny Craig, aka Matt Lucas. I also trained as a hypnotist in my Master NLP Training; not a lot of people know that.

Hypnosis is very useful in sales, actually incredibly useful in sales and few of my training groups know that I'm teaching them hypnotic influencing skills. Would they run a mile if they knew? Instead, I call it "influencing under the radar"; it just sounds cooler.

But back on the subject of matching, let me explain how Joe Vitale explains it, and it'll make absolute sense to you as it did with my group.

Joe, in his book "Buying Trances", talks about egos. Buy the way; it's a great book; you might purchase it. Joe says that everyone has egos, some bigger than others. And all my life, I've met influencers with egos, it goes with the trade, and some argue that is an essential trait of influencers. I don't know. I totally agree with this, but they have a point.

Please let me continue.

NLP teaches us to match our customers to get on their wavelength because people like to deal with people who are like themselves and this is true. But simply matching body language, gestures, voice, and language is, quite frankly, demeaning. Who's Frank?

No, it's deeper than this but not complicated. Fret not; I'm not going to wallow in theory here; that's often the problem with this sort of thing.

I have an ego, just ask my wife, and you have one too; we all have one, even our customers. To a degree, they're important things; they give us self confidence, sometimes too much, assuredness, and self-esteem. All good things. But if you get stuck in yours, you're doomed. We all need to come out of our egos.

And when I explained this to my sales group, they didn't know how to, but they do, really, do you?

And when you're out of your ego, you just need to go into your customers because they'll have one too. And when you're in their ego, see where they are, become like them, think like them, understand them, hear them, enter their ego.

Then you're in rapport.

So the secret is to accept that our ego is not that important; theirs is. I promised I wouldn't wallow in theory; this is really quite simple; simple things in life are the best…just ask my wife.

How Does Hypnotic Selling Work?

So how does it work? Normal hypnotism aims to put someone into a voluntary deep trance where embedded suggestions can be made to help them give up smoking, lose weight, run the marathon, forget about pain and so on.

Hypnotic selling involves a trance, a very low level that is induced mostly by conversation. This conversation and some actions relax the customer and occupy their front mind, known as the conscious or active mind.

Meanwhile, we embed suggestions and ideas into the back of their mind, into their subconscious. It's here where decisions are made and emotions are felt to buy your product, service, or idea that you want your staff member to take on board.

Is it justified?

Well that depends on you. Personally, I believe it is since I believe wholeheartedly in what I sell. I'd buy it myself and if you believe the same about your product, service or idea… then something that will move things to a conclusion is a good thing.

Besides, conversational hypnosis is designed to help the customer understand you, talk freely about their needs and issues and reach a decision whether to buy or not. You're not forcing it down their throats; they still make the ultimate decision, with a little bit of hypnotic persuasion. So if you have a little devil in you… read on to discover the secrets of professional hypnotic selling.

Sleep Little Baby

Hypnotic sales techniques you can use now.

I am a big fan of hypnotic sales techniques. Admittedly, it's not everyone's cup of tea but if your intentions are sound, your morals solid and you are trustworthy, then why not since it speeds up the sales process.

After all, your customer's attention spans are so minute now, anything we can do to shorten the cycle, the better.

To understand hypnotic influencing, you want to be aware of the manner in which it works. Bombard the conscious mind with normal things – language, words, conversation, visual images – you know the usual influencing stuff. This occupies the conscious mind.

Meanwhile you slip in commands through the back door right into the back of their mind, so they do not have time to process them through the front door, which changes things, believe me.

There is nothing better than to settle down to watch a modern cartoon movie. On holiday this year, I watched Puss in Boots, a fantastic film and full of double entendres. You know these kinds of films appeal to children and adults alike because they have two messages going at once – one for the child and one for the adult. Many lines have two meanings but only one meaning is picked up by the viewers – hopefully the right one for them.

In the same way, that is how we sell hypnotically. Double meanings in our language.

Let me show you some techniques to spring forward your hypnotic influencing.

Trance

The best way to bombard the conscious mind is to put the customer into a low-level trance. Think glued in front of Downton Abbey when the best bit happens. Not Derren Brown on the big stage – that is for hypnotists, we're just doing low trancing.

Rapport

You need huge elements of this – read my articles on NLP rapport building, that'll hit the spot.

Voice

Whatever your voice sounds like now, change it. Make it deep and slow. That's it, simple. Deepen it one notch on the octave scale and slow down – a lot.

Relax them

Use trance based language liberally in your speaking. Trace words will put the customer into a mild trance. Some words which bring on a trance:

Imagine – is a great one because you can use this easily in your words; "Imagine what it'll feel like in 2 months' time". "I'd like you to imagine waking up in the morning knowing that your investments are growing in value."

Sleepy words such as – relax, unwind, calm down, slow down, loosen up, settle down, rest assured…zzzz. If you suggest sleep, then people will act and go into trance.

Encourage them

"That's it…that's right…it is within your budget."

Take control

Give the customer instructions, tell them what they should be doing. Show them where to sit down, say what you want them to think, you'll be amazed how receptive they will be.

Agree with them all the way

Use agreement language, after all, everyone likes to be right but then add your point.

"I agree with you on that one…and I would add also…"

"Yes you're right, that's right…another angle is…"

Pink

Wear pink if you can. A pink tie, blouse, shirt. Pink is known to have soporific qualities. It's to do with us becoming accustomed to a pink sunset and sunrise which has anchored warm, relaxing, safe feelings in us since time began.

Take action

As always you have to do something. Let me help you do this because you'd like a neat plan wouldn't you, since this will help you begin hypnotic influencing yet remain full of morals and integrity as I only show those people these little secrets. Have fun.

Oh, I almost forgot, take one a day and bring it into your influencing for that day. The next day, use another. Practice until it becomes second nature and don't start dangling a clock-watch or encouraging people to stare into your eyes – that's nonsense.

Help Me Please

Sssshh, don't tell anyone but this tip is a little hypnotic.

Don't you love a secret?

Here's the tip. Next time you have to ask your customer for some information because the regulations or the procedure requires…use the phrase, *"Help me"*.

"Help me please Mr Brown, could you confirm your address for data protection purposes?"

"Mr Brown, could you help me please, with your email address?"

Humans are wired to provide help if it's asked for. It's hypnotic.

I use it whenever I need to ask for something.

"Could you help me please?" drops all barriers and ensures your customer is alert and ready for your request.

Useful tip don't you think?

A Good Space

End of school holidays, Sunday lunch, Archer household, deepest Gloucestershire.

"So Bethan, are you looking forward to starting in big school next week?"

"Yes Daddy, lots. I'm looking forward to seeing all my old friends and making new friends."

"That's lovely Boo, that's a wonderful thought you have in your head. You hold onto that."

"I will Daddy, I will. How can I do that Daddy?"

"I'll show you how. Before that, show me where that wonderful thought is...point to it, baby."

"It's there, Daddy."

Bethan pointed upwards to her right. And I'd discovered where my daughter puts her good feelings.

Now this is particularly useful to me now, but let me explain first why.

You see people put things in places in their heads, it's how folk roll. Ask them a question to allow them to look in their good place direction, Bethan's was front right slightly upwards. This allows you to influence them hypnotically in a number of ways.

For example, if you want them to feel good about your sales proposal, then place it in their line where good thoughts happen. Easy.

Or move into a position where they see you in their "happy" place and your message will be joyfully received.

And you could even find out their bad space and talk about the competition whilst in that space.

Useful, don't you think?

And for Boo, she's aware of her good place and can put all her thinking there especially going to big school and meeting all her new friends. Just have to be ready for the real impact of big school with 2,500 pupils in one building. Good job I know where her good place is.

Guide Them With Your Hand

This is so clever and sooo hypnotic. Now let me explain how. For a hypnotic meeting, casually lead the customer – use words like:

"In a moment...we'll do this shall we?"

"Now let me explain why..."

People just love to be given direction and have their hands held.

Talking about hands, use your favourite hand to agenda sell. Tell the customer four things you're going to do by pointing to your thumb and first three fingers. Then latch each part of the agenda to the relevant digit and use this digit when you're at that part of the meeting. When they understand something you could raise your finger and ask them if they got your point.

Leave the little finger for your close, this little finger is the commitment digit. You could mention this at the beginning. "We'll leave my little finger for later shall we as you might want to make a decision today, but we'll see later."

Tease them a little, it's fun.

Ask Permission

Have you ever watched stage hypnotists in action? They're great aren't they, but have you witnessed that they always set things up deliberately before they put people in a trance? They ask for permission to hypnotise people and this suggestion is the perfect way to get someone to enter into a trance state voluntarily. They continually ask permission to do things. "Is it OK for you to sit down on this stool?"

For a truly hypnotic influencing meeting, set things up by asking for permission. "Can I sit down"? "Is it OK for me to run through these with you?" "Is it fine for me to speak with you for 10 minutes now?"

Set things up as well as the stage hypnotist. Get to your meeting room early, arrange it so you are sitting with a blank wall behind you in the apex of the room, have everything ready.

All these strategies will help you align the customer with you so you can softly move into sales mode because, you're right...people want and need your product, service or idea.

Do the Bill Clinton

I'm sure you remember Bill Clinton, the President of the United States during the 1990s. He was probably the smoothest president of all time and had a knack of building rapport with almost anyone he met. Use his hand shake technique to good effect. Bill would reach out with his right hand to shake and then subtly use his left hand to touch or hold the elbow of his new friend. This would say to them, "I'm a nice guy, you can trust me, I like you".

You see touch is a very personal thing and not to be encouraged in sales. But the one place which is public is the spot between your elbow and your shoulder. And that's where Bill would touch. Very clever and very subtle. And it worked every time.

Can I Come in Please?

I've left the best one to last. You'll like this. I picked this tip up many years ago as a salesman for a life assurance company. When approaching a customer with the intention of being invited into their home, I would always gesture by wiping my feet on their doormat.

Now I didn't have dirty shoes but it was the physical movement and gesture that just asked for me to come in. It worked every time.

I used it the other day when visiting a client in their offices. It's a gesture that just hypnotises people to say, "Of course, please come in". Try it...it does work. Next time you want to be invited in somewhere, just do the movement with your feet and watch as your customer is slowly hypnotised to say, "Oh...do please come in."

Begin mirroring with the handshake.

We mostly all shake hands with our customers. Of course we do, but do you use this as an opportunity to start calibrating your customer and begin the mirroring process?

Offer your hand by subtly moving it from your side by about 6 inches; this is a very subliminal gesture for the other person to shake your hand, but enough not to get embarrassed if they don't.

Shake and measure their pace and get in tune with their rhythm at this stage. Calibrate their pace and match it. Match their squeeze and tempo of the shake.

On the subject of tempo, continue to gauge them as a person and match their pace, energy, voice and personality. Match their language and use their words, their preferred language and style. Find out their hot buttons, i.e. how they tick, know what's important to them.

Softening Your Commands

Have you ever received a cold call and you just knew that the person was reading from a script? They were full of fantastic promises about saving you money and providing an expert service so why don't you want to buy their product? They seem to think that our saying 'yes' should be a no-brainer.

This kind of arrogance needs to be stamped out completely.

On the phone to Sky recently -- now here's a company that so should lose their monopoly of digital television, because they come over as just so believing they're the best. If you ever try to leave them, they come out with phrases such as, "we're the very best"... "you'll definitely want to come back to us once you've tried the competition"... "you'll get the best service from us."

Instead, try to soften your commands; after all, no one wants to be told what to do all the time.

For example: "Yes, I'm confident we can drive your costs down, but first can I ask some questions?"

Sounds very, if not too, confident. Instead use...

"We might be able to bring your costs down here. Maybe I can find out. Ok if I ask some questions?"

Use phrases such as might, maybe, could rather than will, definitely, certainly. Try them and you'll relax the customer further and build on the trust and rapport.

3-Part Convincers

The magic of this hypnotic closing skill is the rhythm of three. Sometimes called triples. The fact is that everything comes in three. Three is a magic number and falls off the tongue smoothly and effortlessly.

The tip here is to only ever give three benefits or three reasons or three advantages.

And when closing you could use the three-part convincer which is a set of three statements, that are without doubt, true and to which most people will find themselves agreeing.

They are a great calming skill and all you're doing here is confirming to the customer what is true in their minds and allowing them to go into a state of comfort where there are no hidden surprises.

Simply say things that are true for the customer.   Keep them global at first such as:

"It's a beautiful day today, isn't it?"

"Parking's a bit tricky in town at this time."

Then later on you could use some truisms you've found out about the customer such as:

"Your family is a real priority to you, aren't they?"

"From the information on the form, you obviously keep yourselves fit and healthy."

"Getting a service that will save you time is important to you, don't you think?"

As the customer relaxes and sees that your product is right for them... introduce some specific truisms such as:

"So you agree your budget for the package is just under £600 per month?"

"You'd like to complete the forms now?"

Notice that I've tagged some of the questions at the end with what we call a 'yes tag'.

Yes Tags

Another great little closing technique is 'yes tags'.

These are little words at the end of the statements to get a positive 'yes' from the customer. These are useful to gain a commitment to move the sale along. Yes tags come in all sorts of shapes and sizes and I just know you've used them before without knowing what they were called... haven't you?

Examples of yes tags...

- Haven't you
- Aren't you
- Don't you
- Isn't it
- Won't you.

Just put one at the end of a truism statement and your customer will want to nod their head in agreement.

But I'm sure you'll agree, won't you, that overuse is dangerous. Chocolate is lovely in small doses - too much and you can become very queasy indeed...

...don't you think?

Sky Sports and Influencing

People do like to be led, if they want to, and if it offers benefits and value.

Yesterday morning at the departure gate at Dubai airport, various people showed me the way. They looked official and guided me. "Come this way Sir please". I dutifully followed and arrived at the gate in no time.

This evening, following my first meal with my family for over a week and a couple of glasses of wine, I made a phone call to Sky to order a film for us all to watch. The agent casually guided me to take 3 months Sports Channel for half price. She hypnotically led me to say yes.

She used yes tags – "You'll want 3 months watching sports, won't you Mr Archer?"

"And half price is a really good deal isn't it?"

"Yes."

And I did.

It's not sorcery or wizardry. It's gentle persuading that's all.

So if you sell a product or service, rather than pitching it or asking for the business, just lead them to a successful conclusion. Use hypnotic language and patterns to slowly drift towards the sale.

Maybe the wine helped my lady agent at Sky, or that I was relaxed after a long journey home and a family meal but I think she sensed the emotion of the time and used her subtle hypnotic influencing skills to help me buy Sky Sports for 3 months.

And with the English Premiership starting shortly and Manchester United now possessing the best manager in the world, can you blame me. But ssshh don't tell Shelley, she doesn't need to know does she?

The Chair – Spatial Anchoring When Presenting

This week I've been running a 3-day workshop here in Tehran for 25 people with lots of activities and exercises sprinkled with the occasional piece of delivery by myself. Now I wanted to anchor various positions on the "stage" to indicate to the group what was going to happen next.

It's called spatial anchoring, which sounds like some form of physical rehabilitation, but it comes from NLP and allows you to change your audience's state merely by positioning yourself in certain parts of the room.

My chair is a bar stool. It allows me to reach up and keep eye contact with all the attendees and ensures they can see me.

I began the day by standing in the middle, giving instructions on the day and presenting information using the slides and flipcharts. But when it was time to give some topic backed by a story, I went to sit on the chair. I tell a lot of stories and use a ton of metaphors to help my attendees understand the content. I use humour in my stories and relate them to their worlds.

It wasn't long before the group had anchored the chair to mean content plus story plus entertainment. All I had to do was sit at the chair, and they all knew they were going to enjoy a story and some new content. I could visibly see them relax and watch me intently.

By the middle of day one, I started to use the chair to debrief the various exercises they were doing. My objective was for them to be vocal, ask further questions and discuss what they learnt from the activity. By sitting in the chair once again, I encouraged them to do just that. And it worked.

So, for the next three days, I sat at the chair when a special piece of content was coming their way and remained there following the various exercises to ensure they were involved during the debrief.

There we have spatial anchoring. In the past, I've used:

- Flipcharts at either side of the room, one for content giving and the other for brainstorming.

- Three positions on large stages – front stage centre for stories and content, front stage right for slide presenting and front stage left for giving instructions for activities

- Middle of the U shape to calm the group down to end an exercise

They all work, and you won't find many presenters using it, its kind of hypnotic after all and not everyone goes with that. But I know you like me and are different and want to be the top of your game.

Handling Conflict in the Workplace

Back in the late 1990s I was working as a corporate trainer for a large insurance company. It was a new job, a great career move and I wanted to prove myself. Our objective was to provide bespoke sales training to the IFA world and I was part of a team of two. I encountered conflict. Not the kind of conflict with guns at dawn, but a disagreement on how we were going to reach our goal as my colleague had a differing point of view.

Mike and I were different people, with varying values and motivations. He was goal driven and wanted to achieve success at all costs. I was too, but wanted to work together as a team.

Both of us had strengths and the ability to overcook them, make them overdone strengths, I guess weaknesses would be a good description. My confidence maybe edged towards arrogance, Mike's assertiveness nudged towards aggression. These triggered each other, and wound us up even more without even realising.

A common situation in business which I'm sure we've all faced at some time.

You see conflict in the workplace is either warranted i.e. the goal is in dispute, or unwarranted, where the route to the goal is in dispute. Mike and I both agreed on the goal, that was why we were employed. It was the route to the goal that we had different opinions on.

We're triggered further into conflict when our value system is attacked, and this is often achieved by the other person using his overdone strengths. Mike's aggression triggered me. My arrogance triggered him. But I thought I was being confident, honest. And I imagine Mike meant to be assertive.

The answer is to diffuse conflict early, recognise when it begins, handle it. As NLP says, the person with the most flexible approach will be the winner.

Let me explain how you can do this.

The Colours and Conflict

The tool I want to use is the Social Styles Colours which we looked at in depth in an earlier chapter.

In a nutshell this instrument shows how people deploy or use their strengths to support and relate to their value system. Your value system is the core of who you are, the rock, the anchor. My values are integrity, honesty, pride – yours will be different. If your values come under attack, this will cause conflict as you attempt to defend your values.

What Triggers Each Colour?

Triggers are occasions, activities or interactions that trigger you into conflict. Have a look at these, and see if they would wind you up or trigger you into conflict:

Blue	Red	Green	Yellow
Exploiting Them	Detail	Interfering	Isolating them
Isolating Them	Emotions	Demanding	Imposing restrictions
Being too direct	Wasting Time	Keeping them in the dark	Promises that can't be kept
Patronising	Ordering them around	Aggression	Being individualistic
Being Insincere	Playing Politics	Questioning their ability	Taking credit
Being Rude to Others	Not Recognising	Micro management	

Back in 2014 I was working with a client over the summer on a really exciting project which was right up my street. I was helping them to devise the sales process and training programme for video based mortgage advisers.

Half way through the project, the goal-posts changed and a new client was installed. She and I immediately clashed. She would micromanage me, question my ability and was very aggressive. As a green, these triggered me to defend my values.

My conflict sequence took over.

The Three Conflict Stages

A conflict sequence is a three-stage affair which progressively gets more intense. Imagine a tornado if you would. Stage one is up high when the storm is evolving, stage two is in the middle of the funnel and stage three is at the bottom where the tornado is chewing up the ground and destroying everything in sight. Stage three is where the damage occurs.

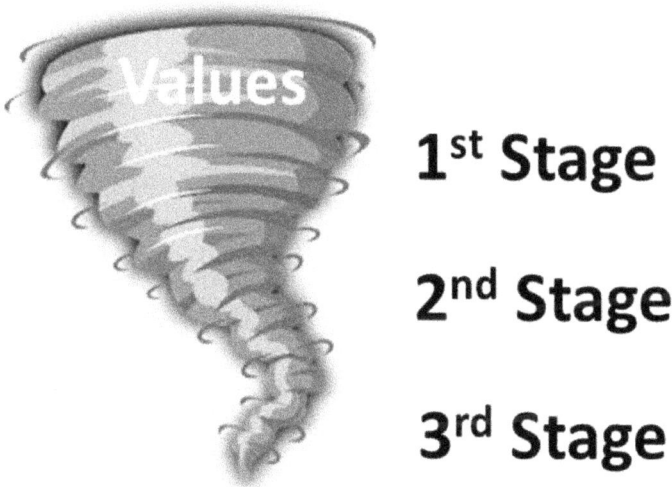

Values

1st Stage

2nd Stage

3rd Stage

The secret is to recognise your stage one conflict both in yourself and the other person and diffuse it. Let's have a quick look at your first stage.

As a green first stage, I analysed with my client what was going on, by going quiet and analytical, trying to figure out what was going on. Blue came next for me, I accommodated her. Finally red kicked in and, being self-employed, I left the client. Thankfully I can do that, but you may not have that luxury.

My sequence is GBR. Green first, then blue, finally red.

Here are the sequences that you have, try and spot yourself:

Stages		Blue	Red	Green
1	Maintain Values	Accommodate	Rise	Caution
2	Preserve Values	Surrender with Conditions	Fight	Retreat to Analyse
3	Challenge to Support	Give In	Claw	Withdraw

As I mentioned earlier the trick to handling the conflict is to diffuse it at stage one, when the damage hasn't yet occurred and the two of you are behaving relatively humanely.

Diffusing the Conflict Stages

Firstly you have to recognise each first stage:

	Red	Blue	Green
How Recognise 1st Stage?	• Voice Faster • Direct Posture • Glaring eye contact • Aggression • Questioning you	• Seeking escape • Seeking compromise • Embarrassment • Taking time	• Go quiet, poker face • Disengage • Lots of questions • Analysing everything

Do you know anyone in your business that displays these traits when entering conflict? I'm sure you do.

Next comes your responses to the conflict. Take care you don't go into your first stage and make things worse. This is what you should and shouldn't do if you want to diffuse the situation. Remember the winner is the one with most flexibility of behaviour.

	Red	Blue	Green
How to Diffuse?	• Meet the challenge • Listen to me talk • Understand my view	• Discussion • Openness • Reassurance • Concede on some points	• Involve us in discussion • Respect opinion • Give space • Give time to think • Be calm
How to Make it Worse?	• Backing off • Going quiet • Disagree with me • Pull rank	• Being dismissive • Arguing • Lack of respect • Belittling	• Talked over • Ignored • Raising your voice • Being too emotional

Conflict Call to Action

Here's your call to action:

1. Know your colour and the values you defend.

2. Know your triggers and try to avoid the impact.

3. Recognise your first stage of conflict.

4. Spot the first stage in your colleague.

Do the right things to diffuse it, don't launch into the first stage yourself, because, inadvertently, that often makes things worse. My client was very red and her natural first stage just wound me up and put me into second stage and so on.

Be the one with the most flexibility.

And my colleague from earlier? We had a three-way meeting with our manager, who acted as an arbitrator to diffuse. We both compromised and got on really well after that event and keep in touch today.

www.ingramcontent.com/pod-product-compliance
Lightning Source LLC
Chambersburg PA
CBHW062007200326
41519CB00017B/4710